CONTENTS

SAUCES AND DRESSINGS

As I passed from aisle to aisle of the Irvine Ranch Market in Los Angeles, the need for this book became quite apparent. My inspiration was the sheer (if not overwhelming) variety of "quick-fix" foods available in virtually every section of the store. First came the ever-growing selection of trimmed, cut and ready-to-cook meats (including skinned and boned chicken breasts, sliced and pounded escalopes of turkey, and tenderloins of everything, even duck breast). Next were the mountainous arrays of seafood on ice. Then followed the artistic displays of fresh pastas in every conceivable shape. And finally, there was a profusion of colorful, garden-fresh vegetables, many of which were newcomers to the salad scene, including radicchio, arugula, baby chicory, mâche, lamb's lettuce and more.

I even asked myself, "Am I being edged out of the cooking process by all these ready-to-toss, -boil, -broil, -sauté and -grill foods? I decided to take advantage of what was before me by giving my culinary talents a stage on which to shine: simply by mastering one of the most interesting parts of a dish—the sauce—and the most inspiring part of a salad—its dressing.

Now, that meant an investment in the finest ingredients like extra-virgin olive oil, which admittedly is expensive, and giving over a portion of the freezer space to little containers and plastic bags filled with flavor-enhancing stock cubes. But that's all. No fancy equipment is required for making even the finest sauces or dressings. And the lengthiest process you will encounter in this book is making stock, for which the recipes have been simplified as much as possible.

Just use your culinary creativity and your taste buds in equal proportion; that's my recipe for making excellent sauces and successful dressings every time.

In all, this book is an offering of opportunities and possibilities, as well as a fresh look at two essential areas of cooking that have been around for just about as long as the urge to eat.

SAUCES AND DRESSINGS

Other books in
The Particular Palate Cookbook™ series

GARLIC
by Sue Kreitzman

RIBS
by Susan Friedland

TAILGATE PARTIES
by Susan Wyler

COOKIES
by Diane Rozas and Rosalee Harris

DELI
by Sue Kreitzman

CHICKEN BREASTS
by Diane Rozas

CHOCOLATE CANDY
by Anita Prichard

COMFORT FOOD
by Sue Kreitzman

FISH STEAKS AND FILLETS
by Michele Scicolone

POTATOES
by Sue Kreitzman

SAUCES AND DRESSINGS

84 Light and Easy Recipes from Nouvelle to New American

BY DIANE ROZAS

A Particular Palate Cookbook™
Harmony Books/New York

For Janelle Cohen, in thanks for her
generous hospitality in New York

A Particular Palate™ Cookbook
Copyright © 1989 by Diane Rozas

Published by Harmony Books, a division of Crown Publishers,
Inc., 225 Park Avenue South, New York, New York 10003.

HARMONY, PARTICULAR PALATE, and colophon are trademarks of
Crown Publishers, Inc.

Manufactured in the United States of America

Library of Congress Cataloging-in-Publication Data

Rozas, Diane.
    Sauces and dressings : 84 light and easy recipes from
nouvelle to new American / by Diane Rozas.—1st ed.
        p.   cm.
    "A Particular palate cookbook."
    Includes index.
    1. Sauces.   2. Salad dressing.   I. Title.
TX819.A1R69   1989
641.8′14—dc19
                                            88-27470
                                            CIP

ISBN 0-517-57117-X
10 9 8 7 6 5 4 3 2 1
First Edition

SAUCES

Contrary to popular belief, no special schooling or genetically derived talent is required to operate a wire whisk and a saucepan, the basic tools of sauce making. And with only a minimum of knowledge and equipment, anyone can whip up a sauce that tastes as if it came from the kitchen of a famous *saucier* (a highly trained cook who devotes all his time to the art of making sauces).

Since ingredients are so very important in creating sauces, let's establish one rule: use nothing less than the best of everything, because ingredients and experience make the difference. And we're not talking about years of experience, either! Once you've effortlessly whipped up a Beurre Blanc for your sautéed breasts of chicken, the truth will be plain. There's nothing to it.

On these pages, you will encounter a broad selection of sauces, from updated classics like Chile Mayonnaise to contemporary contributions such as Spicy Salsa Butter. A few necessities in the Dessert Sauces chapter include Chocolate Sauce Extraordinaire and Chantilly Cream. The Sauce Basics chapter includes many lighter, more flavorful sauces that complement rather than cover up whatever they accompany. Also included here are basic barbecue sauces from Texas and the Orient, a perfect Italian Fresh Tomato Sauce and a luscious sampling of cloudlike butter sauces. So, on with the sauce!

SAUCE BASICS

A FEW WORDS ABOUT TECHNIQUES

CHIFFONNADE: A technique of cutting leafy vegetables and herbs into ribbonlike strands. Roll the lettuce, spinach, collard greens, herbs, arugula, baby chicory, cabbage and so on in a tight bundle, leaf around leaf around leaf. Holding the leaves together tight, slice to the required thickness, usually ¼ to ½ inch. After the bundle has been cut, the result is a pile of curled strips. Vegetables can then be sautéed (as with spinach or collard greens) or used raw as a bed for many different types of salads.

DEGLAZE: A means of using the fat and juices left in the pan after sautéing or roasting to make a pan sauce. First pour off any excess fat from the pan. Add 1 cup of dry white or red table wine, cream or stock to the bubbling juices. Cook over medium heat, stirring constantly and scraping up any brown bits left on the bottom or sides of the pan. Then add enough liquid to the pan (either wine, cream or stock) to make the amount of sauce required. To thicken the sauce, add beaten egg yolks mixed with a little heavy cream, making sure the heat is turned to very low. (Do not boil once the egg yolks have been added.) Strain before serving.

EMULSIFY: When three basic ingredients—an acid (lemon juice or vinegar), a protein (egg yolk) and a fat (butter or oil)—are joined together to hold a light but thick consistency, as with mayonnaise or Hollandaise sauces. In most cases, the oil or butter should be added to the egg yolks very slowly, drop by drop in the beginning, then in a very thin stream, allowing the ingredients to become one, or to emulsify.

JULIENNE: A technique for making very thin strips of food—vegetables, chicken breast, citrus rind and so forth—either for fast-cooking methods or for garnishes. First cut the food into 1½-inch lengths. Pile them together and cut the slices into *very* thin strips.

PURÉE: Using a blender or food processor fitted with a steel blade to process ingredients until they are smooth. Small amounts of food, especially vegetables such as carrots and spinach, purée better in a blender. Try making a pesto sauce in the blender by puréeing the garlic, then adding the basil leaves a few at a time, blending the pesto to a smooth paste with no lumps or flecks.

CLARIFIED BUTTER: Butter with milk solids removed; it is pure fat. In a 1-quart saucepan, heat 1 cup (or more) unsalted butter over low heat until it melts and the milk solids separate from the fat, about 12 to 15 minutes. Remove the pan from the heat and let it stand 1 or 2 minutes before skimming off the foam. Slowly pour off the clear butterfat into a clean container. Discard the residue that has settled in the bottom of the pan. Refrigerate covered. (Lasts indefinitely refrigerated.)

ROASTED AND PEELED PEPPERS:
Roasting is a way of removing the skins from peppers. For sweet red or green peppers, cook for 10 minutes under a broiler set on high, turning frequently, to blacken all sides. For chiles, blacken directly over the burner flame until charred on all sides. Place sweet peppers or chiles immediately in a brown bag or double plastic bag, tightly seal and keep in bag for 10 minutes so the steam will loosen the skins. Peel, remove the seeds, core and devein. (Hot chiles such as jalapeños remain more potent when the veins are left in.) Rinse if necessary and pat dry; cut into sections as required. Store in the refrigerator in a covered glass container. Always wear rubber gloves when handling hot chiles.

REDUCE:
A means of thickening a sauce by cooking ingredients over high heat to decrease the amount of liquid (stock, water, wine or cream), thereby strengthening and concentrating the flavors.

A FEW WORDS ABOUT INGREDIENTS

BOUQUET GARNI:
A French term that refers to an assortment of herbs, spices and aromatic vegetables bound together in a cheesecloth bag and tied with a piece of kitchen string. It is often added to stocks and poaching liquids to impart a concentration of flavors. Typically included in a bouquet garni are sprigs of parsley or thyme, bay leaf, peppercorns and sometimes allspice berries or whole cloves. Celery and leek tops can also be included. Always remove the bouquet garni and discard after the stock or sauce is done.

BLACK AND WHITE PEPPERCORNS:
These are for the most part interchangeable in cooking, except that ground black pepper leaves little black specks, which are undesirable in light-colored sauces. In those cases use white pepper. White pepper is simply a peppercorn without its black outer covering and is slightly more potent in taste.

BUTTER:
Always use unsalted butter (also called "sweet" butter). Butter is frequently used as a binding ingredient to make the sauce shiny, velvety and thick. Unsalted butter imparts a subtle, delicate flavor, allowing the aromatic flavors of herbs, spices and vegetables to become one. Not only does unsalted butter lack salt, but it has fewer milk solids and less water content than salted butter, making it preferable for clarifying (see techniques page 8 for Clarified Butter).

OIL: Use peanut, safflower or corn oil when vegetable oils are called for, and extra-virgin olive oil for dressing salads or in marinades. Virgin or pure olive oils are best for sautéing or cooking. (See Dressings chapter.)

SALT: Coarse salt and sea salt are pure, with no iodine or chemicals added to aid the pouring process. You may need to put this type of salt in a mill and grind it as you would peppercorns each time salt is required. It is superior in taste to regular table salt.

WINE: White and red wines are called for in many recipes. The rule of thumb is simply this: If you would sit down with a glass of the wine or serve it to your best friend, then it is good enough for your sauces. Usually, drier wines are more desirable in sauces. Champagne, when called for, should be brut.

THE SAUCE MAKER'S PANTRY

Use the highest quality ingredients for making sauces. And since you will be using certain of those ingredients over and over again, here's a list of items you might want to keep in your cupboard.

FOODS IN BOTTLES AND CANS
Anchovies
Chiles
Olives (tree-ripened)
Soy sauce (tamari)
Tomatoes (Italian plum)
Tomato paste

PACKAGED AND DRIED FOODS
Almonds
Hazelnuts
Pine nuts
Walnuts
Sesame seeds
Pumpkin seeds
Chiles

COOKING AND DRESSING OILS
Extra-virgin olive oil
Vegetable oils—peanut, safflower, corn, light sesame

WINES AND LIQUEURS
Brandy
Cognac
Champagne (brut)
Sherry (dry and medium)

Vermouth (dry)
Quality dry red and white wines

HERBS AND SPICES
Fresh and dried herbs—tarragon, chervil, marjoram, basil, thyme, bay leaf, etc.
Cinnamon, ground
Chutney (Major Grey's)
Curry powder (Madras)
Ginger, ground
Mustards—Dijon-style and coarse
Nutmeg, whole
Paprika
Peppercorns—black and white
Red pepper flakes
Sea salt

FRESH AND FROZEN FOODS
Unsalted butter
Carrots
Celery
Garlic
Onions
Potatoes
Shallots
Homemade stocks

A FEW WORDS ABOUT EQUIPMENT

FOOD PROCESSOR/BLENDER: Use to chop, purée and blend as well as to create certain emulsion sauces—for example, Béarnaise or mayonnaise.

KNIVES: A well-balanced, French-style knife, with a strong, broad, pointed blade shaped straight at the heel and tapering to a sloping, curved tip is recommended. Another handy item is a paring knife. Both the blade and tip are useful in cooking.

SAUCEPANS: Be prepared to spend some money—$25 to $75—for a pan with a heavy, thick base that will prevent foods and fats, like butter, from burning over high heat. Make sure handles are firmly attached with rivets rather than screws or welding. Pans should have tight-fitting covers. A good choice is stainless steel, which is nonreactive to acids such as tomatoes, vinegar and lemon juice. Heavy-gauge aluminum is the most common, and aluminum pans with stainless-steel linings are ideal.

WIRE WHISK: Sauce whisks are elongated and have no "give," which makes for easy stirring as a sauce thickens. A small wire sauce whisk is perfect for combining dressing ingredients, too.

PEPPER MILL: You could easily have three of these on hand at all times for sauce making—indeed, for cooking in general: one with white peppercorns, one containing black peppercorns, and a mill for coarse salt (non-iodized). Even a fourth, with an interesting combination of black peppercorns and allspice berries (10 parts to 1), is useful.

STRAINERS: A conical-shaped chinois is perfect for straining sauce directly into a serving bowl. A large fine-mesh strainer or colander lined with several layers of cheesecloth will strain stocks. Also, a very fine mesh small strainer is handy for straining lemon or lime juice into a sauce, or straining a small amount of sauce directly onto food.

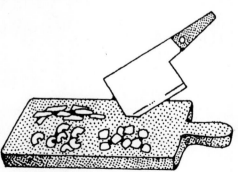

Stocks and Sauces

SIMPLE CHICKEN STOCK

Always keep the ingredients covered with water throughout the simmering process. Do not allow the stock to boil or it will turn cloudy.

Makes about 4 cups

2 pounds chicken parts, including necks and backs
6 cups cold water, or more as needed
1 celery stalk, coarsely chopped, tops included
1 carrot, peeled and quartered
1 onion (skin on), root end cut off
1 leek, coarsely chopped
Bouquet garni (page 10) consisting of parsley, bay leaf, thyme sprigs, peppercorns, cloves (optional)

1. In a 4- to 6-quart non-aluminum stockpot, combine the chicken parts and enough cold water to cover. Over medium heat, slowly bring to a boil, reduce the heat and simmer 45 minutes. Frequently skim off the foam that collects on the surface. (A well-skimmed stock will be clear when chilled.) Remember, do not boil.

2. Add the celery, carrot, onion, leek, bouquet garni and more water if necessary. Simmer over low heat, partially covered, for 3 hours or until the stock is very flavorful.

3. Remove the stockpot from the heat and, with a slotted spoon, take out the vegetables. Discard. Pour the stock through a fine mesh strainer, or a colander lined with a double layer of dampened cheesecloth, into a clean, non-aluminum pot, pressing the bones to extract all the liquid. Cool the stock to room temperature. Refrigerate, uncovered, for 24 hours or up to 4 days.

4. With a spoon, remove the layer of yellow fat from the top. Freeze in individual containers of about 1 cup each, or make into stock cubes (page 19).

BOILED BONES!

That is what the magnificently flavored liquid "stock" is all about. But if it has an intimidating sound, denoting hours of preparation in a hot, steamy kitchen, this simple definition could change the whole picture. A stock is just a savory broth, created by simmering meat, poultry, or fish bones with aromatic vegetables and herbs.

There are several kinds of stock: brown, white, fish and vegetable. White stocks—including chicken and veal—are clear and more delicate than brown stocks. Brown stocks are made with beef or veal bones, roasted or browned in the oven first to obtain a golden color and rich deep flavor before being simmered with aromatics and water. Stock can conveniently be made into tiny cubes and neatly tucked away in the freezer (see "Making Your Own Stock Cubes", page 19).

One thing to remember is that stock is never seasoned with salt because it imparts flavor, not saltiness. Add salt and pepper to a finished sauce, to taste.

FAST FISH STOCK

Nothing goes better with fish than a sauce made with fish stock. Chicken or veal stocks don't mix with the delicate flavors of the ocean's bounty. Egg, cream, wine-based sauces and butter-and-herb sauces are delectable. Homemade fish stock enhances them one and all!

Makes about 4 cups

2 tablespoons (¼ stick) unsalted butter
1 pound bones and trimmings from any
    fresh, white fish (such as sole, flounder,
    whiting), including heads, skin, bones
    and flesh
1 onion, sliced
1 celery stalk, cut into 1-inch pieces, tops
    included
6 sprigs parsley
1 carrot, peeled and cut into 2-inch pieces
2 tablespoons fresh lemon juice
½ lemon, juiced
1 bay leaf
1 sprig dill
½ teaspoon salt
4 cups cold water, or more as needed
1 cup dry white wine

1. In a 4- to 6-quart enamel or non-aluminum stockpot, melt the butter. Combine the bones and trimmings, onion, celery, parsley, carrot, lemon juice, lemon half, bay leaf, dill and salt. Cook over medium heat for 5 minutes.

2. Add the cold water and the wine. Bring to a boil, lower the heat and simmer for 35 minutes. Frequently skim the scum that collects on the surface. Make sure the ingredients are completely covered with liquid during cooking. Do not boil.

3. Strain through a fine-mesh strainer or a colander lined with a double layer of dampened cheesecloth, pressing the bones to extract all the liquids. Freeze in individual containers of about 1 cup each, or make into stock cubes (page 19).

GARDEN VEGETABLE STOCK

Spa cuisine has had an enormous impact on food, especially for those who are interested in improving their health and staying trim. This stock recipe from chef Kim Hutchenson at the Golden Door Fitness Spa is used in place of meat or chicken stock in spa and vegetarian dishes and can be a soup base as well. Add plenty of herbs and no salt.

The combination of ingredients depends totally on what vegetables are available.

Makes about 10 cups

In any proportions you wish:
Zucchini
Broccoli
Turnips, peeled
Onions, quartered
Celery, quartered, tops removed
Carrots, peeled and quartered
Garlic cloves
Bay leaf
Fresh herbs, such as stems of parsley, lemon basil, thyme, or rosemary
Black peppercorns (10 or more)
Whole cloves (2 to 5)
Nutmeg, freshly ground
Sweet peppers (green, red and yellow)
10 cups cold bottled spring water, or more as needed

1. Place the ingredients in a 4- to 6-quart stockpot. Pour in the cold water, bring to a boil, lower the heat to very low and gently simmer for at least 3 hours. Do not allow the stock to boil or it will turn cloudy. (Some cloudiness cannot be avoided with vegetable stock.) The vegetables should remain covered with water throughout the cooking process.
2. Cool to room temperature and strain through a fine mesh strainer or colander lined with a double layer of dampened cheesecloth. Do not press on the vegetables.

3. Refrigerate for up to 1 week or freeze in small quantities. Do not reduce vegetable stock or it will turn cloudy and bitter.

VERSATILE VEAL STOCK

Always make sure the bones are covered with water and the stock is cooking at a *simmer*, not a boil, so you don't end up with liquid that is cloudy and emulsified with fat. Cool the stock to allow it to gel. If it does not, additional cooking may be necessary. When you buy bones, ask the butcher to cut them into many rounds about 1½ inch thick or less, exposing as much of the interior as possible.

Makes about 6 to 8 cups

5 to 6 pounds veal bones, cut into 1½- to 2-inch pieces
3 carrots, peeled and cut into quarters
3 onions, peeled and quartered
¼ cup tomato paste
12 cups cold water, or more as needed
2 celery stalks, cut into 2-inch pieces, tops removed
1 leek, coarsely chopped
Bouquet garni (page 9) containing parsley, thyme sprigs, bay leaf and black peppercorns

1. Preheat the oven to 450° F.

2. Place the veal bones, carrots, onions and tomato paste in a large roasting pan. Roast about 40 minutes or until browned. Turn once during roasting.

3. Remove the bones and vegetables to a non-aluminum stockpot. Pour the fat from the roasting pan. Deglaze the pan with 1 cup of the water and bring to a boil over medium heat, scraping the sides and bottom with a spatula to loosen the brown bits. Pour the mixture over the bones and vegetables, and add the remaining cold water. The bones should be covered by 3 to 4 inches. Add more water if needed.

4. Slowly bring the water to a boil, reduce the heat and simmer for 1 hour. Frequently skim the scum that collects on the surface.

(A well-skimmed stock will be clear when chilled.)

5. When no more scum rises to the top, add the celery, leek and bouquet garni. Simmer the stock, partially covered, over low heat for 8 to 10 hours or overnight. (The surface should show only an occasional bubble breaking.) The bones should remain completely covered with water during the cooking process. Remember, do not boil.

6. When the stock is done, pour the liquid through a fine-mesh strainer, or colander lined with a double layer of dampened cheesecloth, into a clean, non-aluminum stockpot. Do not press on the ingredients.

7. Cool the stock to room temperature. Refrigerate, uncovered, for 24 hours or up to 4 days. Remove the layer of solid fat from the top. Bring the stock to a boil and reduce to about 2 quarts or less. Freeze in individual containers of about 1 cup each or make into stock cubes (page 19).

WHITE OR LIGHT VEAL STOCK
Omit the roasting process in steps 1 and 2, and eliminate the tomato paste. Begin with step 3 and continue as directed. Skim the stock often.

THE SECRETS OF A MASTER STOCK MAKER

Stock is everything to a sauce. Time is everything to a stock," chef-saucier Thierry Rautureau said.

Every morning, starting at 7 A.M., Thierry, executive chef at the Seventh Avenue Bistro in Los Angeles, makes chicken stock, tomato-based veal stock and duck stock. "Stock requires long, slow simmering of the ingredients. I put in leftover stems of parsley; herbs such as thyme, tarragon and bay leaf; even leftover greens of leeks; carrots, onions and celery; but not zucchini or turnips, as they will purée during cooking and cloud the stock. In a restaurant, we cook stock from seven in the morning until eleven at night. Once it has cooked, it can stay in the refrigerator for days, or be frozen indefinitely. Once you have it, you can make all kinds of basic sauces, like beurre blancs, very fast," Thierry said.

Tasting Thierry's red wine sauce, made with veal stock, was a special treat. And during the making of that stock, he passed on these pearls of wisdom. "The best bones to use in veal stock are the shank bones—they have lots of gelatin. Brown the bones *very* well in the oven. Add the vegetables, and after they are browned, add the tomato paste. Cooking the tomato paste in this way removes some of the acidity. After all the ingredients are well browned, fill the pan with water and simmer on top of the stove. Always add salt when you are making the sauce, not in the stock. When you're making chicken stock, make sure you don't cook in aluminum or the stock will become grayish; and always keep the bones covered with water," he advised.

POACHING LIQUID

This recipe is used for all types of fish and shellfish. After poaching, the liquid is strained and reduced over high heat until only 2 to 3 tablespoons remain, then it is added to a sauce for an extra boost of flavor.

1 cup dry white wine
1 cup water, or more as needed
2 to 3 shallots, or 1 onion, quartered
½ carrot, peeled and thinly sliced
1 celery top, chopped
1 leek (white part only), coarsely chopped
4 to 6 black peppercorns
Pinch of salt

In a poacher or large stockpot, combine all of the ingredients and bring to a boil. Proceed as directed in the individual recipes.

MAKING YOUR OWN STOCK CUBES

After the stock is cooled and the excess fat is removed from the surface, it can be boiled to reduce it down to half its original volume. At this point, the stock can be divided among small 1- to 2-cup containers and frozen. Or continue to boil the stock until it is about one-fifth of its original volume. Pour the stock in plastic ice-cube trays and freeze. When frozen, transfer the cubes to lock-top plastic freezer bags and freeze until needed.

To make a further reduction of veal or chicken stock to a *glace* (an intensely concentrated stock cube), continue boiling down the liquid, transferring it to smaller and smaller saucepans. (This reduction process is important in order to have greater and greater control of your stock, with less surface evaporation.) Pour the reduced stock onto a jelly-roll pan and let stand. When the *glace* begins to harden, freeze it, then cut into cubes and store in lock-top plastic freezer bags until needed. (The *glace* of veal stock typically will be harder than that of chicken because of its higher gelatin content.)

BÉARNAISE SAUCE

This is made much like Hollandaise, except that the yolks are flavored with a reduction of wine, vinegar, shallots and fresh tarragon. It is especially good on hamburgers, broiled or sautéed fillet of beef, or grilled tuna or swordfish.

Makes about 1 cup

1 cup dry white wine
2 tablespoons white wine vinegar
¼ cup finely chopped shallots
1 tablespoon chopped fresh tarragon, or 2
    teaspoons dried
2 egg yolks
1 cup (2 sticks) unsalted butter, melted and
    cooled to lukewarm
Salt and freshly ground white pepper

1. In a small saucepan over medium-high heat, reduce the wine, vinegar, shallots and tarragon until only about 2 to 3 tablespoons remain. Strain the liquid into a metal bowl.

2. Add the egg yolks to the wine reduction. Place the bowl over the pan of simmering (not boiling) water, making sure the bottom of the bowl is not touching the water. Whisk about 4 minutes or until pale in color and thick.

3. Pour in the melted butter in a thin but steady stream, whisking continuously until the sauce has thickened. Season to taste with salt and pepper. Serve immediately.

TOMATO Substitute melted, clarified butter (page 8) for regular, unsalted butter. In a small sauté pan over medium-high heat, cook 1 peeled, seeded and chopped tomato and ¼ teaspoon salt until almost all the moisture has evaporated. Stir into the finished Béarnaise sauce.

GINGER BÉARNAISE Make the Béarnaise sauce omitting the tarragon. Add 2 tablespoons peeled and finely grated fresh ginger to the finished Béarnaise sauce.

HOLLANDAISE SAUCE

Fear not! Anyone can make this famous French sauce, one you've probably enjoyed a dozen times before over eggs Benedict or asparagus spears. It's downright simple to make and very versatile. See the variations that follow for some delicious new ideas.

Makes about 1 cup

3 egg yolks, at room temperature
2 tablespoons water
1 cup (2 sticks) unsalted butter, melted and hot
2 to 3 tablespoons fresh lemon juice
Salt and freshly ground white pepper

1. In a metal bowl, combine the egg yolks and the water. Whisk until well mixed.

2. Place the bowl over a pan partially filled with hot water, making sure the bottom of the bowl does not touch the water. Over low heat, whisk for about 4 minutes or until the mixture thickens. (Make sure the water is not too hot or the eggs will scramble, in which case you must begin again with fresh egg yolks. If the water begins to simmer, immediately add some cold water and remove the bowl momentarily.)

3. When the egg yolks are creamy and thickened, remove the bowl and gradually add the melted butter, starting with a few drops at a time, then adding the remaining butter in small amounts, whisking constantly.

4. After all the butter is incorporated and the texture of the sauce is light, stir in the lemon juice, salt, and pepper to taste. Serve immediately.

NOTE To keep warm for 15 minutes (no more), place over the pan of warm water, or pour the sauce in a Thermos that has been rinsed first with warm water and dried well. Cover the sauce with a piece of plastic wrap to keep a "skin" from forming. If the sauce is too thick, whisk in 1 tablespoon warm water. If it is not smooth, or if bits of egg are visible, strain through a fine-mesh strainer.

WINE Add 2 tablespoons fortified wine (vermouth, Madeira, Marsala, port, sherry) to the sauce after the butter has been incorporated. Serve with meat, chicken or fish.

MUSTARD Add 2 to 3 tablespoons Dijon-style mustard to the finished Hollandaise. Serve over broiled fish or roasted chicken.

CAPER Add 1 tablespoon rinsed and drained small capers to the finished Hollandaise. Serve with fish, poultry or eggs.

HERB Add 1 tablespoon any chopped fresh or 1 teaspoon dried crushed herbs to the finished Hollandaise. Serve over puff pastry shells filled with sautéed wild mushrooms.

BASIC REDUCTION SAUCE

Note the versatility of this easy-to-make butter sauce by checking out the delicious flavor variations and their suggested accompaniments.

Makes about 1 cup

½ cup dry white wine or stock
2 tablespoons minced shallots
½ cup heavy cream
4 tablespoons (½ stick) well-chilled unsalted
    butter, cut into 8 or more small pieces
Salt and freshly ground white pepper

1. In a heavy, medium sauté pan over medium-high heat, reduce the wine or stock and shallots by half, or until about 4 tablespoons remain.

2. Add the cream and continue reducing over high heat for about 2 minutes, or until the bubbles forming around the sides of the pan are thick and shiny.

3. Remove the sauté pan from the heat and begin whisking in the butter, 1 piece at a time, adding each new piece of butter just before the previous one has completely melted into the sauce. Work quickly.

4. Season to taste with salt and pepper. Serve immediately, or keep warm according to directions on page 21.

HERB Instead of plain butter, substitute herb butter. (See Flavored Butters, page 25.) Serve with steak or lobster.

FRUITY Instead of plain butter, substitute fruit butter. (See Flavored Butters, page 25.) Serve with sautéed chicken breasts.

MUSTARD Whisk 1 tablespoon Dijon-style mustard and 1 tablespoon coarse-grain mustard into the sauce after the butter has been completely incorporated. Serve over sautéed chicken or broiled shrimp.

ROSEMARY Add 1 teaspoon very finely chopped fresh rosemary to the wine and shallots. Continue as directed. Serve with pork.

PESTO Whisk in 2 to 3 tablespoons Pesto (page 29) after the butter has been incorporated. Serve with fresh poached or broiled tuna, swordfish or pasta.

ROASTED RED PEPPER SAUCE Roast 2 sweet red peppers (page 9). In a food processor fitted with a steel blade, purée the peppers. Warm the purée and whisk into the sauce after the butter has been incorporated. Serve over grilled or steamed vegetables.

TOMATO AND BASIL Add 2 tablespoons lightly chopped fresh basil leaves to the reduction in step 1. Peel, seed and chop 1 ripe tomato. Warm the tomato, then whisk into the sauce after the butter has been completely incorporated. Serve with poached eggs or pasta.

LIME Eliminate the wine from the recipe. Sauté the shallots in 1 tablespoon unsalted butter for 2 minutes. Add ¼ cup fresh lime juice and 3 tablespoons port wine to the shallots and reduce by half. Decrease the amount of cream in the recipe to ¼ cup, add to the shallots, then bring to a boil for 1 minute to reduce slightly. Continue as directed in step 3. Finish with a pinch of cayenne (ground red) pepper. Serve with any type of delicate fish filets.

RASPBERRY Eliminate the wine and shallots from the recipe. In a sauté pan, reduce ¼ cup raspberry vinegar, ¼ cup crème de cassis and 2 tablespoons brandy as directed in step 1. Eliminate the cream in step 2; instead, add 1 cup chicken or veal stock to the sauté pan and reduce to about 4 tablespoons. Continue as directed in step 3. Add freshly ground black pepper instead of white to finish. Serve with veal, chicken, duck or even game.

BUTTER SAUCES

Basic Reduction Sauce and Beurre Blanc are made smooth and their volume increased by whisking pieces of chilled butter into a concentration of flavors called a "reduction" (ingredients that have been reduced in quantity over high heat, and can include wine, cream, vinegar, spices, stock, shallots and herbs).

It is essential to use well-chilled butter, added in small pieces over very low heat, and to continuously whisk while adding the butter to ensure a silky, smooth texture. Flavorings such as lemon juice, dill, ginger, horseradish, basil, tarragon, orange juice, fruit, pesto and so on can be added to the finished sauce (see variations following each recipe).

Be ready to serve your butter sauce as soon as it's done, because reheating causes the soft butter to melt and the sauce to fall apart. However, the butter sauce can be kept warm for 15 minutes (no more) when the pan is placed over a bowl of *warm* water, or pour the sauce into a Thermos that has first been rinsed with warm water and then dried well.

Though the technique for making both of these sauces is the same, the real difference is in the amount of butter: Beurre Blanc requires about twice as much as the Basic Reduction Sauce.

BEURRE BLANC

This light but rich sauce can be partnered with many main-course favorites, such as breast of chicken, duck and turkey; steamed vegetables; and fresh pasta.

Makes about 2 cups

½ cup dry white wine or stock
2 tablespoons white wine vinegar
2 tablespoons finely chopped shallots
1 cup (2 sticks) well-chilled unsalted butter, cut into 16 or more small pieces
Salt and freshly ground white pepper

1. In a heavy, medium saucepan over medium-high heat, reduce the wine or stock, vinegar and shallots until only about 3 tablespoons of liquid remain. Remove the saucepan from the heat and cool slightly.

2. Whisk in 2 pieces of butter until the sauce is soft and creamy. Just before the first 2 pieces of butter are incorporated, add 2 more and continue in this manner until all the butter has been completely incorporated. Work quickly and remember to whisk vigorously to make the sauce high and light.

3. Add the salt and pepper to taste. Serve immediately or keep warm according to directions on page 21.

NOTE If necessary, begin to heat the pan slightly over low heat for a few seconds about halfway through adding the butter. Be careful not to use too much heat or the butter will melt and the sauce will lose its stability. The bottom of the pan should never be hot to the touch.

BEURRE ROUGE Instead of white wine and white wine vinegar, substitute ½ cup dry red wine (Beaujolais, Zinfandel or other good-quality red table wine) and 2 teaspoons red wine vinegar. Continue as directed.

ORANGE Add the juice of 2 fresh oranges and 1 tablespoon blanched orange zest to step 1. Continue as directed. Sprinkle a pinch of zest over the top of the sauce when serving.

BALSAMIC Instead of white wine and white wine vinegar, substitute ¼ cup balsamic vinegar and ⅓ cup dry red wine. Continue as directed. Serve over steamed spinach, topped with toasted chopped walnuts.

SAVE THAT SAUCE!

If your Beurre Blanc loses its stability or "turns," it can be saved. Combine 1 to 2 tablespoons cold water and 1 tablespoon firm butter in a clean saucepan and whisk over low heat for 30 seconds until well combined. Slowly add this mixture to the sauce, whisking constantly over low heat for 1 minute. Beat in 3 to 4 tablespoons of fresh butter. When the sauce is smooth and thick again, readjust the seasoning.

FLAVORED BUTTERS

Flavored butters are the simplest of all sauces; they require no cooking and can be prepared in advance. Use them straight from the freezer on steamed vegetables, grilled fish, sautéed meats, basted chicken or even a dish of plain rice or pasta. An omelet cooked in flavored butter is fantastic. To prepare, combine all the ingredients in a food processor fitted with a steel blade. Process or blend until smooth. (For Walnut and Herb Butter, stir in walnuts after blending.) Shape the butter into a 1-inch-thick log on a piece of plastic wrap. Wrap tightly and freeze. Cut off pieces as needed. In addition to the following, experiment with such flavor possibilities as tarragon, curry, garlic and chives and lemon- mustard butters. For biscuits, try strawberry-cinnamon butter—even chocolate, for croissants.

WALNUT AND HERB BUTTER
1 cup (2 sticks) unsalted butter
1 tablespoon fresh parsley, minced
2 tablespoons fresh herbs, minced (thyme, dill, basil, tarragon or a combination of several herbs)
2 tablespoons chopped fresh chives
1 small garlic clove, minced
Salt and freshly ground black pepper
¼ cup walnuts, coarsely chopped

ANCHOVY BUTTER
1 cup (2 sticks) unsalted butter
2 tablespoons fresh lemon juice
6 anchovy filets, rinsed, dried and finely chopped
2 tablespoons chopped fresh chives

DEVIL'S BUTTER
1 cup (2 sticks) unsalted butter
1 teaspoon Dijon-style mustard
2 teaspoons grainy-style mustard
Scant ½ teaspoon prepared horseradish
1 teaspoon crushed garlic
1 teaspoon green peppercorns, rinsed and finely minced

LIME BUTTER
1 cup (2 sticks) unsalted butter
2 tablespoons dry white wine
2 tablespoons half-and-half
2 tablespoons fresh lime juice
1 tablespoon grated lime zest

FRUIT BUTTERS
1 cup (2 sticks) unsalted butter
2 tablespoons dry white wine
½ cup crushed berries (blueberries, apricots, peaches, strawberries, raspberries or other fruit)

FRESH TOMATO SAUCE

"It's basic, healthy, fresh, quick to make; it freezes perfectly, but it's a crude sauce," says chef Tim Dobrovolskis. "By adding a touch of butter, the acid quality is removed. To make a finished sauce, sauté bacon and onions with some crushed red pepper flakes; add this, along with a dash of garlic oil (olive oil infused with garlic cloves) and a splash of white wine, to several cups of Fresh Tomato Sauce. Then pour the sauce over ziti or linguini.

Makes 4 to 6 cups

6 pounds Italian plum tomatoes
⅓ cup olive oil
8 garlic cloves
1 tablespoon *very* finely chopped fresh
    rosemary
¼ bunch fresh basil
1 carrot, scrubbed, not peeled
Pinch of salt and freshly ground black
    pepper (scant amount)
1 cup tomato purée (canned or imported in
    the tube)
1½ cups dry white wine

1. Score the tomatoes with a paring knife, making an X at the core end. Plunge into boiling water until the skins start to separate.

Pull the tomatoes from the water, peel and chop into little pieces. (Some texture is needed, so do not chop them too fine.

2. In a large sauté pan or heavy skillet over medium-high heat, add the olive oil and the garlic. Cook for 2 to 3 minutes, until the garlic is brown, not black. Remove and discard. Add the tomatoes, rosemary, basil, carrot, salt, pepper and tomato purée.

3. Bring the mixture to a boil and then add the wine. Let boil for 1 minute. Turn the heat down to low and simmer for 1 hour, skimming the reddish scum that collects on the surface several times.

4. Bring the sauce to room temperature. Store in the refrigerator, covered, for up to 1 week.

TOMATO SAUCE TIPS

- Use fresh, ripe Italian plum tomatoes, which have very little water content. Round tomatoes are too mealy.

- Grind or chop the tomatoes after peeling, saving chunks. Texture is needed in this sauce but not inconsistent pieces or strands.

- Go easy with the pepper, especially if chiles will be added later to the sauce.

- Freeze the sauce in plastic ice-cube trays. Use 2 cubes per serving when making sauces.

SPICY RED MEXICAN SALSA

Salsa is typically served with chips as a dip in Mexico and at most Mexican restaurants this side of the border, too. Use it as a condiment, also. For spicier salsa, increase the number of hot chiles to three.

Makes about 3 cups

4 large fresh tomatoes, peeled
2 serrano or jalapeño chiles, stem and seeds removed (page 9)
3 small red onions, quartered
4 small garlic cloves
5 tablespoons fresh cilantro leaves, finely chopped
6 teaspoons red wine vinegar or lemon juice
1 tablespoon salt

A CHILE NOTE

It is always wise to wear rubber gloves when working with potent hot chiles. The hot oil contained within the chiles will quickly penetrate the skin, burning for hours later. No amount of water or ice will cool this flame. Wash all work surfaces and kitchen equipment after coming in contact with these fiery little devils. *Never* rub your eyes or face while working with hot chiles.

1. In a food processor fitted with a steel blade, chop the tomatoes. Transfer to a medium bowl.

2. In the food processor, combine the chiles, onions and garlic. Process until finely minced. Transfer to the bowl with the tomatoes.

3. Mix in the cilantro, vinegar or lemon juice, and salt. Taste for seasoning. Refrigerate for 3 hours before using or up to 3 days.

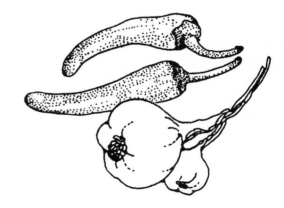

"WOE TO THE COOK WHOSE SAUCE HAS NO STING."

—CHAUCER

27

SAVORY SABAYON

Makes about 3 cups

1½ cups stock (fish, chicken or white veal
    stock)
3 egg yolks
1 cup (2 sticks) well-chilled unsalted butter,
    cut into 16 pieces

1. In a small saucepan over medium-high heat, reduce the stock until only about 5 or 6 tablespoons remain. Let cool.

2. In a large metal bowl, combine the egg yolks and stock. Whisk until well mixed. Place the bowl over a large pan partially filled with hot water, and set over low heat. (The water should be steaming but not simmering, and the bottom of the bowl should not be touching the hot water.) Continue whisking vigorously for about 10 minutes or until the mixture thickens.

3. Whisk in the butter, about 4 pieces at a time. With each addition, make sure that the butter is completely incorporated into the sauce before the next amount is added. When the sauce is thick and foamy, stop adding more butter. Pour into a warmed sauce bowl and serve immediately.

SWEET SABAYON

Makes about 3 cups

½ cup superfine sugar
6 egg yolks
1 cup white Sauternes, Champagne, Marsala
    or medium-dry sherry

1. In a large, heavy saucepan, combine the sugar and egg yolks. Whisk until well mixed. Place the saucepan over a large pan partially filled with hot water, and set over low heat. (The water should be steaming, not simmering, and the bottom of the bowl should not be touching the hot water.) Whisk the egg yolks and sugar together until the mixture is creamy and pale yellow in color.

2. After the sugar is dissolved, add the wine, whisking constantly. The mixture will slowly froth up into a mousse, doubling in volume after about 10 minutes. The sauce should be very light and foamy.

3. Serve warm in parfait glasses, over cakes or cold. To chill quickly, pour the sauce into a metal bowl set into a larger bowl filled with ice cubes, and whisk constantly until cold.

PESTO

Makes about 1½ cups

3 to 4 large garlic cloves
1 large bunch fresh basil, stems removed
2 tablespoons pine nuts
½ cup extra-virgin olive oil
1 cup freshly grated pecorino cheese (Italian
　　sheep's milk cheese) or imported
　　Parmesan

1. Purée the garlic using a blender or food processor fitted with a steel blade.

2. Add the basil leaves and very finely chop or blend until well combined with the garlic. Add the pine nuts until finely chopped.

3. Add the oil a little at a time to make a paste. Add the cheese just before serving. Store in a container in the refrigerator or freezer with a thin film of oil over the top.

SABAYON

Unlike most other sauces, Sabayon can be sweet or savory. This rendition of the feather-light sauce is ideal for steamed vegetables and poached fish. Sweet Sabayon, a beautiful, pale-yellow sauce, is similar to a custard. Spoon it over cake, fresh poached fruit or berries. One Italian version, *zabaglione*, is served solo in a parfait glass; it is usually flavored with interesting liqueurs and can also be folded into whipped cream to make a richer mousseline sauce. Fold in beaten egg whites to make the sauce stiffer.

What's more, Sabayon is a breeze to make. But don't let the egg yolks become too hot while beating them over the pan of hot water or they will scramble or, worse, cause the sauce to curdle and separate during the cooking process. In either case, the only remedy is to throw out the mess and start from scratch.

SAUCES LOVE HERBS

Herbs are as common as cabbage when it comes to putting them in sauces. Among these saucy herbs are the ubiquitous parsley, fragrant sage, recognizable rosemary, basil, tarragon, oregano and venerable bay.

Herbs that are long-cooked in sauces will impart a greater intensity of flavors. A perfect example is stock, to which a bouquet garni is added in the beginning and remains until the stock is done.

On the other hand, last-minute additions of herbs yield lighter flavors, such as the classic French combination called *fines herbes*—chives, chervil, parsley and tarragon—which add a certain snap to quick-cooking lighter sauces.

Preserving fresh herbs for sauce making in seasons to come is highly advisable. When the fresh herbs are in full swing, purée the greener ones (basil, parsley, dill, mint) separately with a bit of olive oil. Then freeze in small containers, or tie great fragrant bunches of herbs such as oregano, tarragon, marjoram, rosemary and so on, and hang them upside down to dry in the kitchen. The sight, and especially the smell, of drying herbs will add a bit of spice to your life as well as to your sauce.

TEXAS BARBECUE SAUCE

Soak shortribs, brisket of beef or chicken pieces in this sauce for a few hours before cooking over a pit of crackling white coals.

Makes about 2 cups

2 to 4 garlic cloves, coarsely chopped
1 small, dried hot red chile, stem and seeds removed (page 9)
1 teaspoon chopped fresh cilantro
¼ teaspoon ground cumin
½ teaspoon anise seed
½ teaspoon salt
2 tablespoons brown sugar
1 tablespoon Worcestershire sauce
1 cup cider vinegar
2 cups catsup
2 to 3 tablespoons Tabasco

1. In a blender or food processor fitted with a steel blade, combine the garlic, chile, cilantro, cumin, anise seed, salt, brown sugar and Worcestershire sauce. Process until smooth.

2. Place the mixture in a medium saucepan and add the vinegar and catsup. Bring to a boil, reduce the heat and simmer, uncovered, for 25 to 30 minutes. Add the Tabasco and cool to room temperature. Place in a tightly covered container and refrigerate up to two weeks.

ORIENTAL BARBECUE SAUCE

Use this complex combination of oriental flavors on barbecued chicken, fish, pork or flank steak. Marinate the meat or fish in the sauce for at least 1 hour, then use it to baste while broiling or grilling.

Makes 2 cups

½ cup peanut oil
¼ cup hoisin sauce
¼ cup soy sauce
½ cup rice vinegar
¼ cup dry sherry
½ teaspoon hot chile oil
2 whole scallions, minced
2 garlic cloves, minced
2 tablespoons fresh ginger, minced

1. Combine all ingredients in a small bowl. Whisk until well mixed. Store in the refrigerator up to two weeks.

PASTAS AND SAUCES

PENNE ALLA PUTTANESCA

This interpretation of the classic recipe is from chef Tim Doborovolskis.

Serves 4

SAUCE
6 tablespoons olive oil
2 garlic cloves, chopped
4 anchovy filets, chopped
2 tablespoons small capers
8 olives (Gaeta, if possible)
⅓ cup dry white wine
1½ cups Fresh Tomato Sauce (page 26)
1 tablespoon chopped fresh parsley

1 pound penne or other pasta of choice
Salt
Freshly grated Parmesan cheese
2 tablespoons chopped fresh parsley

1. In a large sauté pan, heat the oil. Sauté the garlic until lightly browned. Add the anchovies, capers, olives, wine, tomato sauce and parsley. Simmer the ingredients for 2 to 3 minutes.

2. Cook the pasta in lightly salted, rapidly boiling water until al dente. Drain well.

3. Add the pasta to the sauce and move the pan back and forth quickly to flip the pasta and sauce together. Serve with a generous amount of Parmesan cheese and garnish with parsley.

RAVIOLI WITH TOMATO SAUCE AND BROWN SAGE BUTTER

This recipe is from chef Tim Doborovolskis.

Serves 4

1½ pounds fresh ravioli, stuffed with cheese, lobster or sausage
Salt

SAUCE
1 cup Fresh Tomato Sauce (page 26)
3 tablespoons unsalted butter
6 fresh sage leaves
Pinch of ground white pepper
Pinch of freshly grated nutmeg

1. Cook the ravioli in lightly salted, rapidly boiling water until al dente. Do not over-cook. Carefully remove the ravioli from the water with a wide slotted spoon. Drain and place in a single layer on a warmed platter.

2. In a saucepan, heat the tomato sauce. Taste for seasoning and adjust if necessary.

3. In a small sauté pan over high heat, add the butter, sage leaves, pepper and nutmeg. Cook until the butter turns brown, but be careful not to let it burn. Remove from heat immediately.

4. To assemble, pour some of the sauce on individual plates. Gently slide several ravioli onto the sauce. Spoon more tomato sauce over the ravioli and pour on the hot browned butter. Divide the sage leaves evenly. Serve immediately.

COLD SESAME NOODLES IN PEANUT SAUCE

Serves 4 to 6

1 pound Japanese *kisoba* (buckwheat) noodles or fresh egg pasta such as fettuccine
Salt and freshly ground white pepper
2 tablespoons dark sesame oil
2 tablespoons light sesame oil
2 scallions (white parts and some of the green), sliced lengthwise into 1-inch pieces

SAUCE
2 tablespoons sesame paste (tahini)
3 tablespoons tamari (Japanese soy sauce)
¼ cup rice vinegar
½ teaspoon sugar
2 garlic cloves
⅛ teaspoon cayenne (ground red) pepper
6 tablespoons peanut butter, or ½ cup roasted peanuts and 1 tablespoon peanut oil
¼ cup water
Salt and freshly ground white pepper
½ cup chopped roasted peanuts, for garnish
3 tablespoons chopped fresh cilantro, for garnish

1. Cook the noodles in lightly salted, rapidly boiling water until al dente. Run cold tap water over the noodles to stop the cooking process. Place in a shallow mixing bowl, and cool to room temperature.

2. Sprinkle the noodles with a scant amount of salt and pepper. Drizzle on the dark and light sesame oils, add the scallions and toss to combine well. Refrigerate, covered, for at least 2 hours or overnight.

3. In a blender or food processor fitted with a steel blade, combine the sesame paste, tamari, vinegar, sugar, garlic, cayenne, peanut butter or peanuts and peanut oil, water and a scant amount of salt and pepper. Blend to a smooth sauce. Add more salt and pepper to taste.

4. Combine the sauce with the noodles and toss. Sprinkle on the peanuts and cilantro, then toss again gently. Serve at room temperature.

LINGUINE WITH PROSCIUTTO AND SUN-DRIED TOMATOES

Serves 4

SAUCE

¼ cup virgin olive oil

¼ cup chopped onion

1 garlic clove, minced

1 tablespoon chopped fresh basil, or 1½ teaspoons dried

¼ teaspoon red pepper flakes (optional)

3 tablespoons chopped sun-dried tomatoes, drained of oil

1½ cups peeled and chopped ripe Italian plum tomatoes

½ teaspoon salt and freshly ground black pepper

⅛ pound prosciutto, cut into julienne strips

1 pound linguini or other pasta of choice

Salt

1. In a medium saucepan, heat the olive oil. Over medium heat, sauté the onion for 5 to 7 minutes, until soft and slightly browned.

2. Add the garlic, basil and red pepper flakes. Cook 1 minute more.

3. Lower the heat and add the sun-dried tomatoes, fresh tomatoes, salt and pepper. Simmer for 15 minutes, stirring occasionally. Add the prosciutto and cook 10 minutes more.

4. Cook the pasta in lightly salted, rapidly boiling water until al dente. Drain well. Place the pasta in a large warmed bowl, pour on the sauce and toss. Serve immediately.

SUN-DRIED TOMATOES

If you've bought Italian sun-dried tomatoes in olive oil lately, you know that these delicacies come with a hefty price tag. Making your own is easy.

When making your own, start with 6 pounds of Italian plum tomatoes, which are lower in water content and have a more concentrated flavor than round tomatoes. Slice each tomato lengthwise but not completely in half, open out like a book and arrange the tomatoes, cut side down, on an oven rack. Sprinkle with salt and place the rack on a baking sheet. Bake in a 225° F. oven until the tomatoes have shriveled to three-fourths their original size. They are done when deep red and warm and dry to the touch—not hard. Cool to room temperature before combining with olive oil and additional flavorings—herbs, garlic, wild mushrooms—if desired. Select attractive jars, equaling 5 cups. Marinate the tomatoes for 4 to 6 weeks at room temperature.

Fry bread in a bit of herbs, oil and butter. Top with Roquefort cheese and bits of sun-dried tomato. And a jar of sun-dried tomatoes makes a unique gift.

Seafood and Sauces

SWEET RED PEPPER ROUILLE

Great with cold boiled shrimp, lobster or shellfish salad.

Makes about 2½ cups

2 large sweet red peppers, roasted, peeled
　　and seeded (page 9)
5 garlic cloves
1 teaspoon saffron threads, soaked in ¼ cup
　　dry white wine for 1 hour
10 drops Tabasco
Pinch of cayenne (ground red) pepper (optional)
1 cup mayonnaise, at room temperature

1. In a blender or food processor fitted with a steel blade, process the red pepper and garlic until puréed. Add the saffron and wine, Tabasco, cayenne and half the mayonnaise. Blend or process to combine thoroughly.

2. Fold the mixture into the remaining mayonaise, and chill before serving.

SAUCING THE FISH OF YOUR FANCY

When making fish, you will find that the sauce usually takes no longer to prepare than the fish itself.

Fish sauces typically include vegetables, herbs, wine and liqueurs, butter, cream, oil and sometimes eggs. Certain flavorings may be added to the basic sauce, like fresh ginger, lemon or lime, sweet red peppers, mustard, leeks, scallions and onions, dill, fennel and horseradish. These flavorings partner perfectly with fish and shellfish, complementing the delicate nature of these foods without overpowering the desirably mild characteristics. If you fancy yourself an intuitive cook, able to create your own sauce recipes as you go along, pick one flavoring and let it dominate the sauce. For example, choose either fresh ginger or lemon, or blend two, like leek and lime, for greater complexity. (Don't forget a splash of white wine—a little something extra for the fish!) But if you would like a more structured approach to making a perfect fish sauce, the recipes on these pages offer some quick, tasty choices. Also, fish loves butter sauces, for which there are recipes in the Sauce Basics chapter.

LIME SOY SAUCE

Try it on shark!

Makes about 1½ cups

⅓ cup soy sauce
2 teaspoons grated lime zest
¼ cup fresh lime juice
2 garlic cloves, minced
1 tablespoon Dijon-style mustard
¼ cup peanut oil
¼ cup finely chopped scallions (white parts
    and a little of the green)
½ teaspoon freshly ground black pepper
3 tablespoons dry white wine
Lime peel, julienned, for garnish

1. In a small bowl, combine the soy sauce, lime zest, lime juice, garlic and mustard. Whisk until mixed well. Add the oil in a thin, steady stream, whisking constantly. Stir in the scallions and pepper.

2. Place the white wine in a small saucepan. Bring to a boil and reduce to 1 tablespoon. Stir in the lime-and-soy mixture. Heat through and drizzle over cooked fish. Garnish with strips of lime peel.

CUCUMBER SAUCE

Perfect along with any cold poached white fish.

Makes about 2 cups

1 large cucumber (hothouse, if available),
    peeled, seeded and thinly sliced
1 teaspoon coarse salt
1 tablespoon minced fresh chives
2 tablespoons white wine vinegar
1 cup sour cream
Salt and freshly ground black pepper
1½ to 2 tablespoons salmon caviar

1. To remove any bitterness from the cucumber, place the slices around the inside of a colander, sprinkle with coarse salt and drain over a bowl for 30 minutes. Rinse, pat dry and finely chop. Place in a mixing bowl.

2. Combine the chives, vinegar and sour cream with the cucumber. Season to taste with salt and pepper.

3. Chill well before serving. Top with a dollop of caviar.

GARLIC WINE SAUCE

Wonderful on white fish or any fish salad.

Makes 1 cup

½ large sweet yellow pepper, cored, seeded
    and chopped
¾ cup dry white wine
¾ cup Fast Fish Stock (page 15)
3 garlic cloves, crushed
Salt and freshly ground white pepper

1. In a saucepan, combine the yellow pepper, wine, stock and garlic. Simmer for about 15 to 20 minutes, until the yellow pepper is very soft and the liquid is reduced to one-third the original volume. Cool slightly.

2. Place the ingredients in a blender and blend until smooth. Add salt and pepper to taste. Chill before serving.

CHILE MAYONNAISE

A wonderfully assertive sauce for cold grilled salmon.

Makes 1½ cups

2 jalapeño chiles, roasted, peeled and seeded
    (page 9)
2 egg yolks
¾ cup peanut oil
1 tablespoon lime juice
1 tablespoon lemon juice
1 sweet green or red pepper, finely diced

1. Mince the jalapeños (page 9). Set aside.

2. In a food processor fitted with a plastic blade, beat the egg yolks. With the motor running, add the oil, starting with just a few drops at a time. Slowly increase the amount to a very thin stream as the oil is completely absorbed into the egg yolks.

3. After the mayonnaise has emulsified, transfer to a small mixing bowl and fold in the minced jalapeños, lime juice, lemon juice and green or red pepper. Refrigerate until ready to use.

STEAMED SEA BASS WITH BLACK BEAN SAUCE

This is the oriental manner of saucing a fish. Simple. A Chinese-style bamboo steamer is required, along with a wok. Any other type of whole fresh fish may be substituted for sea bass, such as red snapper, pompano, striped bass or sea trout.

Serves 4

SAUCE
2 teaspoons cornstarch
2 tablespoons medium-dry sherry
1 tablespoon peanut oil
¼ cup minced fermented black beans (available in jars)
1 tablespoon minced fresh ginger
1 tablespoon minced garlic
¼ cup scallions (white and green parts), cut in ⅛-inch pieces
⅔ cup Simple Chicken Stock (page 14)
1 tablespoon oyster sauce (available in jars)
2 teaspoons soy sauce

1 to 1½ pounds sea bass, scaled, gutted and fins removed
1 tablespoon medium-dry sherry
1 tablespoon dark sesame oil, for garnish
3 tablespoons chopped scallions (mostly green parts), for garnish

1. In a small bowl, mix the cornstarch and sherry. Set aside.

2. Heat the oil in a wok over high heat until very hot but not smoking. Add the black beans, ginger, garlic and scallions. Stir-fry for about 15 seconds. Add the chicken stock, oyster sauce and soy sauce. Bring to a boil and reduce for about 2 minutes.

3. Pour in the cornstarch mixture, stirring constantly until the sauce thickens. Transfer the sauce from the wok to a small saucepan. Set aside.

4. Fill the bottom of the wok with water and bring to a boil. Place the bamboo steamer over the top of the wok. (The water should not be touching the bottom of the steamer.)

5. Place the whole fish in an ovenproof dish that fits loosely inside the steamer. Place the bowl in the second tier of the basket, leaving the tier closest to the water empty. Steam the fish for at least 10 to 12 minutes. Do not overcook.

6. Place the fish on a heated platter. Reheat the black bean sauce. Remove from the heat, stir in the sherry and sesame oil, stir and pour the sauce over the fish. Garnish with scallions. Serve immediately.

POACHED SEA SCALLOPS IN TOMATO-DILL SAUCE

Serves 4

Poaching Liquid (see page 19)
1 to 1½ pounds fresh sea scallops

SAUCE

2 ripe tomatoes, peeled, seeded and diced
¼ teaspoon celery seed
2 sprigs fresh dill, stems removed and tops
    chopped
2 tablespoons (¼ stick) unsalted butter
Salt and freshly ground black pepper

1. In a medium sauté pan, bring the poaching liquid to a simmer. Add the scallops and poach for about 3 to 4 minutes or just until done. Do not overcook.

2. Transfer scallops to a warmed platter and cover with foil.

3. Strain the poaching liquid into a saucepan. Over high heat, reduce by half. Add the tomatoes, celery seed and dill. Cook for 3 minutes, then remove the pan from the heat, add the butter and quickly whisk to incorporate. Season to taste with salt and pepper.

4. Slice the scallops in half. Arrange on plates and spoon on the sauce. Serve immediately.

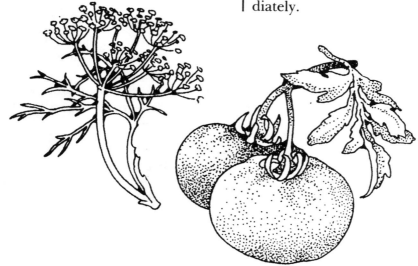

GRILLED SWORDFISH AND SALSA BUTTER

During the grilling process, give the fish a quarter turn to create the cross-hatch pattern that suggests "food cooked over coals." This pattern has come to symbolize outdoor-style cooking, and most recently, Western and Southwestern styles of cooking as well.

Consider substituting fresh Hawaiian ahi, the fish for which this recipe was originally created at Shep Gordon's oceanside abode on the island of Maui.

Serves 4

1 to 1½ pounds swordfish steaks
Salt and freshly ground white pepper
¼ cup olive oil
Juice of 1 lemon
Juice of 1 lime
4 sprigs cilantro, stems removed and leaves
    chopped
3 tablespoons coarsely chopped fresh parsley

SAUCE
½ cup (1 stick) unsalted butter
½ cup Spicy Red Mexican Salsa (page 27)

1. Place the swordfish in a shallow glass pan. Sprinkle with a little salt and pepper. Drizzle on the olive oil and lemon and lime juices, and sprinkle with the cilantro and parsley. Cover the pan with plastic wrap. Marinate the fish for up to 4 hours in the refrigerator.

2. In a small sauté pan, melt the butter. Add the salsa and swirl together. Set aside.

3. Prepare the grill with charcoal and wood chips such as mesquite, if desired. When the coals are very hot, remove the swordfish from the marinade. Place the fish on paper towels to absorb the oil and remove most of the cilantro and parsley. Grill about 6 to 8 inches away from the heat for 4 to 5 minutes per side. Do not overcook.

4. Place the grilled fish on a serving platter. Pour on the sauce. Serve immediately.

CRAB CAKES WITH GARLIC TARTAR SAUCE

Makes 10 cakes/20 for appetizers

SAUCE

2 cups mayonnaise
2 teaspoons garlic purée
2 teaspoons small capers, drained and
 crushed
2 tablespoons very finely chopped fresh
 herbs, or 2 teaspoons dried herbs (such
 as tarragon, savory, thyme, oregano,
 sage, marjoram, rosemary, basil)
2 tablespoons chopped sour gherkins or
 nonsweet pickles
2 tablespoons lemon juice
Few drops Tabasco (optional)
1 tablespoon Dijon-style mustard
2 tablespoons chopped fresh parsley
2 teaspoons chopped pimiento, for garnish

1 pound fresh lump crab meat (about 2½
 cups), carefully picked to make sure no
 pieces of shell remain
2 eggs, well beaten
2 cups fresh bread crumbs
1 teaspoon Dijon-style mustard
2 tablespoons finely chopped fresh parsley
¼ cup finely chopped onion or chives
¼ cup heavy cream, whipped just until
 thickened
Vegetable oil for frying

1. In a small bowl, combine the mayonnaise with the garlic purée, capers, herbs, gherkins or pickles, lemon juice, Tabasco and mustard.

2. Cover the bowl and refrigerate for at least 4 hours. Bring to room temperature and just before serving, stir in the parsley. Garnish with pimiento.

3. Place the crab meat in a large mixing bowl. Add the eggs, 1½ cups of the bread crumbs, mustard, parsley, onion or chives, and cream. Blend carefully, trying not to break the pieces of crab apart too much.

4. Shape the crab mixture into 10 balls (20 for appetizers). Press each into a patty shape about ¾ inch thick.

5. Coat the patties with the remaining bread crumbs. Fry in as little oil as possible, 3 minutes on each side or until browned. Flatten to ¼ inch thick during cooking. Absorb any excess oil with paper towels. Serve hot with the tartar sauce.

POULTRY AND SAUCES

CHICKEN BREASTS WITH TARRAGON SAUCE

Elegant party fare!

Serves 4

SAUCE

3 shallots, chopped
2 tablespoons chopped fresh tarragon
½ teaspoon freshly ground black pepper
⅔ cup dry white wine
¼ cup tarragon wine vinegar
3 drops Worcestershire sauce
1½ cups heavy cream

2 whole chicken breasts (about 2 pounds
    total), skinned and boned
Salt and freshly ground white pepper
2 tablespoons (¼ stick) unsalted butter
⅓ cup dry white wine

1. In a small saucepan over medium-high heat, cook the shallots, tarragon, pepper, wine, vinegar and the Worcestershire sauce for 10 minutes, or until the bottom of the saucepan is almost dry and only about 2 to 3 tablespoons of liquid remain. Stir in the cream. Set the pan aside.

2. Season the chicken breasts with salt and pepper. Flatten slightly with the palm of your hand.

3. In a sauté pan or heavy skillet over medium-high heat, melt the butter. Sauté the chicken breasts for 2 to 3 minutes on each side or just until lightly browned. Do not overcook. Remove to a plate.

4. Pour the wine into the sauté pan and reduce over high heat until most of the moisture has evaporated.

5. Lower the fire, add the sauce, return the chicken breasts to the pan and continue cooking, turning occasionally, for about 7 minutes or until the chicken breasts are tender. Remove to a heated platter. Season with salt and pepper if needed, and spoon the sauce over the chicken breasts. Serve immediately.

ROAST CHICKEN WITH SWEET CURRY SAUCE

Sliced roast turkey or chicken breast can be substituted. Heat the cooked fowl in the curry sauce and serve buffet style with an array of condiments such as raisins, shredded coconut, additional chutney and steamed rice.

Serves 4 to 6

1 roasting chicken, about 3 to 4 pounds
Salt and freshly ground black pepper
2 yellow onions, quartered
1 tablespoon dried herbs, such as sage, savory, basil, tarragon, rosemary or parsley
2 tablespoons (¼ stick) unsalted butter, melted

SAUCE

3 tablespoons unsalted butter
½ cup minced onion
3 tablespoons all-purpose flour
1 tablespoon curry powder (Madras, if possible)
1 teaspoon salt
1 teaspoon sugar
½ teaspoon finely minced fresh ginger
¼ cup unsweetened shredded coconut
1 cup fresh coconut milk
1 cup milk
¾ cup Major Grey's chutney, chopped

1. Preheat the oven to 325° F.

2. Sprinkle the inside of the chicken with salt and pepper. Fill with the onion quarters and herbs. Baste with butter and roast, uncovered, for about 10 minutes per pound (or according to package instructions).

3. In a medium sauté pan, melt the butter. Over medium heat, sauté the minced onion for 5 minutes or until tender. Sprinkle on the flour, curry powder, salt, sugar, ginger and coconut; mix well.

4. Stirring constantly, pour in the coconut milk and the milk. Reduce the heat to very low, and cook for about 30 minutes or until the sauce is thick. Stir in the chutney.

5. Cut the chicken into serving portions. Arrange pieces on a platter and spoon on hot curry sauce. Serve the soft onions and herbs in a dish on the side along with the remaining curry sauce.

FRUITY CURRY SAUCE After the onions are tender (step 1), add 1 peeled, cored and grated green apple; 1 thinly sliced banana; and 1 cup fresh pineapple chunks. Continue as directed, substituting 1 cup homemade chicken stock for the milk. Eliminate the chutney, if desired. After the sauce is done, purée in a blender. Serve hot over chicken or turkey.

ESCALOPES OF GRILLED TURKEY BREAST WITH PARSLEY AND SHALLOT SAUCE

This inventive recipe comes from one of Los Angeles's most popular new restaurants—City Restaurant —and was developed by chefs Susan Feniger and Mary Sue Milliken.

Serves 4 to 6

2 tablespoons (¼ stick) unsalted butter
2 bunches collard greens, trimmed, washed and cut into chiffonnade
Salt and freshly ground black pepper
½ turkey breast (2½ pounds), trimmed, sliced across the grain into small escalopes and pounded into ¼-inch-thick pieces about 8 ounces each
½ cup all-purpose flour, for dusting
2 to 3 tablespoons clarified butter or rendered chicken fat, for quick frying

SAUCE

5 to 6 shallots, finely diced
1½ tablespoons lemon juice
3 tablespoons chicken stock
3 tablespoons very cold butter, cut into small pieces
1½ tablespoons finely chopped fresh parsley
Salt and freshly ground black pepper

1. In a sauté pan over medium-high heat, melt the butter. Quickly sauté the collard greens for about 2 minutes, shaking the pan back and forth to gently toss while cooking. Season with a little salt and pepper. Remove to a warm bowl. Set aside.

2. Season the turkey escalopes with a scant amount of salt and pepper. Lightly flour the turkey, shaking off any excess until almost no flour remains. Set aside.

3. Heat a heavy cast-iron skillet or stovetop grill until very hot. In a heavy sauté pan, heat the clarified butter or chicken fat to very hot. Quickly cook each piece of turkey in the skillet or on the grill, turning after 30 seconds. (Do not overcook as the turkey dries out almost instantly.) Transfer to the skillet with the hot fat and briefly sauté the escalopes about 10 seconds on each side, or just long enough to cook the flour. Set aside and keep warm.

4. Add the shallots to the pan in which the collards were cooked and sauté quickly over medium-high heat for about 2 minutes or until tender.

5. Add the lemon juice and stock, then increase the heat to high and reduce by half. Remove the pan from the heat and add the cold butter, one piece at a time, whisking vigorously to incorporate each piece before adding the next. Stir in the parsley. Season to taste with salt and pepper.

6. To assemble, make a bed of collard greens on each plate and arrange the escallopes of turkey on top. Spoon the sauce over the turkey. Serve immediately. Pass any remaining sauce in a bowl.

SAUTÉED CHICKEN BREASTS WITH GINGER SAUCE

Serves 4

2 whole chicken breasts (about 2 pounds total), boned, skinned, flattened to about ½ inch and halved
Flour for dredging
Salt and freshly ground black pepper
3 tablespoons peanut oil
2 tablespoons grated fresh ginger
¼ cup finely chopped scallions (white parts and some of the green)
1 cup chicken stock

SAUCE
2 teaspoons cornstarch
3 tablespoons medium-dry sherry
3 tablespoons soy sauce
Salt and freshly ground black pepper
2 tablespoons coarsely chopped scallions (green parts only), for garnish

1. Dredge the chicken breasts in the flour and shake off any excess. Sprinkle lightly with salt and pepper.

2. In a large sauté pan, heat 2 tablespoons of the oil. Over medium-high heat, sauté the chicken breasts for 2 to 3 minutes or until lightly browned. Do not overcook. Place on a heated platter to keep warm.

3. Add the remaining tablespoon of oil to the pan. Turn the heat to medium, then add the ginger and the scallions. Sauté just until softened. Add the stock and bring to a boil, lower the heat and cook for 2 minutes more.

4. In a small bowl, combine the cornstarch, sherry and soy sauce; add a few drops of water to make a smooth mixture. Add cornstarch mixture to the sauté pan and cook, stirring constantly, for about 30 seconds or until the sauce thickens. Season with salt and pepper if needed. Pour over the chicken breasts, garnish with scallions and serve immediately.

Meats and Sauces

SEARED SIRLOIN WITH ROQUEFORT SAUCE

Serves 4

1 to 1½ pounds sirloin steak, 1½ inches thick, trimmed of all visible fat (flank steak can be substituted)
Salt and freshly ground black pepper
1 tablespoon vegetable oil

SAUCE
1 tablespoon unsalted butter
4 shallots, minced
2 garlic cloves, minced
¾ cup Simple Chicken Stock (page 14)
¾ cup dry white wine
1¼ cups heavy cream
½ cup crumbled Roquefort cheese

1. Place the meat in a heavy skillet, and sprinkle with salt and pepper. Add just enough of the oil to keep the meat from sticking to the pan. Sauté over high heat for 3 minutes on each side. Slice thinly on the diagonal, and arrange the pieces on a warmed platter. Place the platter in a warm oven.

2. Over medium-low heat, melt the butter. Add the shallots and garlic, and cook just until tender.

3. Add the stock and wine to deglaze the pan. Increase the heat to high and reduce by half. Add the cream and reduce again by half.

4. Lower the heat, add the cheese and continue stirring until it melts. Transfer the mixture to a blender and purée. Rewarm over low heat or in a double boiler.

5. Arrange the sirloin pieces on individual plates, and top with hot sauce. Serve immediately.

STILTON OR GORGONZOLA SAUCE Instead of Roquefort cheese, substitute Stilton or Gorgonzola.

RED WINE SAUCE Using the same skillet in which the meat was seared, pour off any excess fat and add ¼ cup chopped shallots, 1 pressed garlic clove, ½ teaspoon black peppercorns, 1 small bay leaf, ½ teaspoon dried thyme and 1 cup quality Beaujolais. Bring to a boil and reduce the ingredients to about 3 tablespoons. Remove the pan from the heat and strain. Melt 12 tablespoons (1½ sticks) unsalted butter, then cool slightly. Slowly drizzle the butter into the sauce, whisking constantly. Season with salt and freshly ground black pepper. Spoon over the meat.

BEEF STROGANOFF

This variation of an old classic is from the City Restaurant in Los Angeles.

Serves 6

2 tablespoons vegetable oil
2½ pounds beef tenderloin, trimmed of all
    fat and sliced into 3-inch rounds
Salt and freshly ground black pepper

SAUCE
1½ cups sliced mushroom caps
Salt and freshly ground black pepper
½ cup dry white wine
1 cup julienned dill pickles
2 teaspoons pickle juice
¾ cup heavy cream

1½ pounds fresh fettuccine
Salt
¼ cup heavy cream
Salt and freshly ground white pepper

1. Place the oil in a large, heavy skillet over high heat. Season the tenderloin with salt and pepper. When the oil is very hot and almost smoking, sear the tenderloin rounds for about 3 minutes on each side or until browned. Remove to an ovenproof platter and place in a low oven to keep warm.

2. In the same skillet in which the meat was cooked, sauté the mushrooms over medium heat for about 2 minutes. Add salt and pepper. Increase the heat to medium-high, add the wine and reduce by half. Lower the heat and add the pickles, juice and cream. Mix well and continue cooking about 5 minutes or until the sauce thickens. Adjust seasoning with salt and pepper.

3. Cook the fettuccine in lightly salted, rapidly boiling water until al dente. Drain and transfer to a saucepan. Add the cream and a pinch of salt and pepper. Heat together for 1 minute.

4. To assemble, divide the fettuccine in mounds among 6 warmed dinner plates. Place the tenderloin rounds on top of the fettuccine and pour on the sauce. Serve immediately.

GRILLED SAUSAGE WITH SWEET RED PEPPER AND MUSTARD SAUCE

Grilling—man's first cooking method—is still on top of a list of popular cooking styles. When the sausage is cut in bite-size pieces, this recipe makes a wonderful grilled appetizer as well as a main course selection.

Serves 4

SAUCE

2 large sweet red peppers, roasted, peeled and seeded (page 9)
1 small garlic clove
½ cup dry mustard
¾ cup boiling water
Pinch of cayenne (ground red) pepper
5 drops Tabasco (optional)
½ cup red wine vinegar
½ cup sherry vinegar
½ cup dry red wine
½ cup medium-dry sherry
1 tablespoon coarse salt
5 black peppercorns
½ teaspoon crushed allspice
1 tablespoon honey
½ teaspoon dried oregano
¾ teaspoon crumbled dried thyme

1½ to 2 pounds medium or hot Italian pork sausage, or chicken or veal sausage

1. In a blender, purée the peppers and garlic. Set aside.

2. In a small bowl, combine the mustard, water, cayenne, Tabasco and wine and sherry vinegars. Whisk to combine thoroughly. Set aside.

3. In a small non-aluminum saucepan, combine the wine, sherry, salt, peppercorns, allspice, honey, oregano and thyme. Bring to a simmer and continue cooking 5 minutes. Remove from the heat and let cool.

4. Strain the sauce, then combine with the mustard mixture. Place in a double boiler and cook until reduced to a thick sauce. Remove the pan from the heat, let cool to room temperature and stir in the red pepper purée.

5. Prepare the grill. Grill the sausages 6 to 8 inches from the heat for 8 to 10 minutes, turning frequently to cook inside evenly. Cut in 2-inch pieces and serve with the warm sauce.

VIRGINIA HAM WITH CUMBERLAND SAUCE

Serve with hot or cold ham. This sauce goes well with meats served at any temperature, as well as with pâtés and roasted game. The classic French sauce is a perfect balance of sweet and tart, with a touch of orange.

Serves 4 to 6

SAUCE

1 shallot, chopped
5 tablespoons red wine vinegar
½ teaspoon coarsely ground white pepper
Juice of 1 orange
½ cup Versatile Veal Stock (page 17)
¼ cup port wine
3 tablespoons red currant jelly
1 teaspoon Worcestershire sauce
Zest of 1 orange or lemon, cut into very fine julienne and blanched for 30 seconds
Salt

Virginia ham or any other precooked ham, 6 to 8 ounces per serving

1. In a small non-aluminum saucepan, combine the shallot, vinegar and pepper. Over high heat, reduce the liquid by two-thirds.

2. Add the orange juice, stock, wine, currant jelly and Worcestershire sauce. Bring to a boil, lower the heat and continue cooking for 20 minutes. Strain the sauce and place in a bowl. Refrigerate.

3. When sauce is cold, combine the orange or lemon zest with the sauce. Season with salt to taste.

4. Slice the ham, arrange on a platter and pass the sauce in a separate dish.

MUSTARD HORSERADISH

SAUCE In a medium bowl, slightly whip ¾ cup heavy cream. When cream begins to thicken, mix in ¾ cup sour cream, ¼ cup drained prepared horseradish, 2 tablespoons Dijon-style mustard, 2 tablespoons coarse mustard, a pinch of salt and a pinch of sugar. Whisk together until well combined. Refrigerate until ready to serve with cold ham, cold rare roast beef or country pâté.

Vegetables and Sauces

ZUCCHINI FRITTERS WITH APRICOT-MUSTARD SAUCE

Serves 4

SAUCE
1 cup apricot preserves
1 teaspoon white wine vinegar
2 tablespoons Dijon-style mustard
Pinch of white pepper

Vegetable oil for deep-frying
2 eggs, separated
½ cup milk
1⅓ cups cornmeal, sifted
2 teaspoons baking powder
¾ teaspoon salt
Pinch of freshly ground black pepper
1 cup shredded zucchini
2 tablespoons minced parsley, for garnish

1. In a small saucepan, warm the preserves. Add the vinegar, mustard and pepper. Place the ingredients in a blender and blend until smooth. Set aside.

2. In a heavy skillet, add oil to a depth of 2 inches. Heat the oil to 375° F.

3. Beat the egg yolks and milk together. Beat the egg whites until stiff peaks form.

4. Sift together the cornmeal, baking powder, salt and pepper. Stir the dry ingredients quickly into the egg-yolk mixture; do not overmix. Heap the egg whites on top of the batter, and fold together gently. Fold in the zucchini.

5. Drop the batter by tablespoons into the hot oil. Turn once, if necessary. When golden, about 3 to 4 minutes, remove fritters with a slotted spoon and drain on paper towels. Serve garnished with parsley and the sauce in a bowl on the side for dipping.

CORN AND ZUCCHINI FRITTERS
In addition to the zucchini, add fresh young corn kernels scraped from the cob. Do not press hard against the cob, only the tender tops should be used. Blanch ½ cup of corn kernels for 30 seconds, drain well, then mix into the batter.

SAUTÉED TOFU WITH FRESH VEGETABLE PURÉE

Tofu is bean curd—very high in protein and very low in calories. It is found frequently in oriental dishes.

Serves 6

SAUCE
¼ cup water
¾ cup dry white wine
⅓ cup diced peeled carrots
⅓ cup thinly sliced celery
½ cup diced peeled tomato
⅓ cup sliced zucchini
½ cup chopped onion
Salt

1 to 1½ cartons tofu (about 14 ounces each), marinated in ½ cup sake (rice wine) and ½ cup chopped scallions
3 tablespoons peanut oil
4 shiitake mushrooms, cleaned and cut into eighths
Florets from 1 piece broccoli, cut into small pieces
1 sprig fresh basil, chopped
1 leek (white part and some of the green), cut in julienne
½ pound fresh medium shrimp (optional), cleaned and deveined

1. Combine the water and wine in a saucepan large enough to hold all the vegetables. Bring to a boil and add the carrots, celery, tomato, zucchini and onion. Reduce the heat to low, cover and cook for 10 minutes. Transfer to a food processor fitted with a steel blade, and purée. Lightly season with salt.

2. Return the purée to the saucepan. Bring to a boil and reduce by one-third. Set aside.

3. Remove the tofu from the marinade. Pat dry with paper towels. Cut into ½-inch-thick slices.

4. Heat 1 tablespoon of the peanut oil in a heavy skillet. Quickly sauté the mushrooms. Add 1 more tablespoon of oil to the pan. When hot, add the broccoli, basil and leek; sauté briefly. Add the shrimp and sauté 2 to 3 minutes more. Do not overcook the shrimp. Place in a warm bowl, cover and set aside.

5. In a heavy skillet, heat the remaining tablespoon of oil. Sauté the tofu for about 3 minutes on each side or until lightly browned.

6. To assemble, place the tofu on a warmed platter. Top with the shrimp mixture, spoon on hot sauce and serve immediately. Pass the remaining sauce in a dish.

SWEET-AND-SOUR SAUCE OVER VEGETABLES AND WILD GRAINS

"This dish is plain, simple, good-flavored and aesthetically clean, with color and texture provided by the vegetable items on the plate," said chef Kim Hutchenson from the Golden Door Fitness Spa. "There was a time when spa cuisine was a little bit of food served in the center of a big white plate. Not so now. This is well balanced and flavorful, and you can have a plentiful serving because calorie-wise it's well balanced, too."

Serves 2 to 4

SAUCE

2 cups Garden Vegetable Stock (page 16) or
    Simple Chicken Stock (page 14)
1 cup chopped celery
¾ cup chopped carrots
1 cup chopped peeled tomatoes
1 teaspoon Chinese five-spice powder
½ tablespoon chopped fresh ginger
½ cup rice vinegar
1 cup unsweetened pineapple juice
2 tablespoons low-sodium soy sauce

3½ cups Garden Vegetable Stock (page 16)
1 onion, coarsely chopped
1 bay leaf
1 sprig lemon thyme
⅛ teaspoon freshly grated nutmeg
4 scallions (white parts only), chopped
1¼ cups short-grain brown rice
¼ cup wheat berries
¼ cup barley
¼ cup wild rice

¼ pound snowpeas
1 each sweet yellow, green and red peppers
1 zucchini, cut into chunks 1½ inches long
4 celery stalks (only the tender smaller
    stalks), cut on the diagonal into
    2-inch pieces
2 cups broccoli florets
2 cups cauliflower florets
Other vegetables in season

1. In a 3-quart saucepan, combine 2 tablespoons of the stock with the celery, carrots, tomatoes, five-spice powder and ginger. Cook over medium heat for 2 minutes.

2. Add the remaining stock, vinegar, pineapple juice and soy sauce. Simmer for 30 minutes over low heat. Cool slightly, then purée in a blender for about 2 minutes or until very smooth.

3. Place a sauté pan over high heat. When very hot, add ¼ cup of the stock. When the stock starts jumping across the bottom of the pan, add the onion. The intense heat will extract the flavor from the onion; cook for about 3 minutes, but do not brown.

4. Add bay leaf, lemon thyme, nutmeg and scallions. Then add the rice and grains to the pan, along with the remaining stock. Cook, covered, over medium heat about 35 to 40 minutes or until done.

5. Steam the vegetables separately, because they have very different cooking times. Steam each until the color is brilliant and the vegetable is tender to the touch with a knife, but not overcooked.

6. To assemble the plate, place the steamed vegetables on a bed of wild grains. Drizzle on the sweet-and-sour sauce. Serve more sauce on the side.

61

EGGPLANT WITH GARLIC SAUCE

Make this dish a day or more in advance for the best flavor. Serve it at room temperature.

Serves 4 to 6

6 dried black Chinese mushrooms, washed
1 cup warm water

SAUCE
¼ cup bottled chili sauce
2 tablespoons medium-dry sherry
2 tablespoons soy sauce
2 tablespoons red wine vinegar
1 teaspoon dark brown sugar, packed
1 teaspoon Szechuan chili paste with garlic
    (measure carefully—very hot)
⅓ cup vegetable or chicken stock

1 eggplant (1 to 1½ pounds), cut into 1-inch
    cubes
2 teaspoons salt
2 tablespoons peanut oil
3 to 4 garlic cloves, minced
3 scallions (white parts and some of the
    green), sliced
1 sweet green pepper, cut into 1-inch pieces

1. Soak the mushrooms in the warm water for 30 minutes or until soft. Drain and reserve mushrooms and soaking liquid.

2. In a bowl, combine the chili sauce, sherry, soy sauce, vinegar, brown sugar and chili paste. Stir in the stock and the reserved mushroom soaking liquid. Set aside.

3. Place the eggplant cubes on a baking sheet. Sprinkle with salt and cover with several layers of paper towel. Place a cutting board or butcher's block on top of the eggplant and let stand 30 minutes. Rinse and dry the eggplant with more paper towels.

4. Squeeze any excess water from the mushrooms into the sauce ingredients and slice mushroom caps into ¼-inch-thick strips. Set aside.

5. Heat the oil in a wok until very hot but not smoking. Add the eggplant and stir-fry for about 3 minutes or until lightly browned.

6. Add the garlic and scallions, and stir-fry for 30 seconds more. Add the mushrooms and pepper pieces and stir-fry about 1 minute or until the peppers begin to soften.

7. Add the sauce ingredients and continue cooking over medium heat for about 1 to 2 minutes more or until the sauce thickens. Store in the refrigerator, covered, up to 24 hours before serving. Serve at room temperature.

Dessert Sauces

CHOCOLATE SAUCE EXTRAORDINAIRE

When this sauce is served over orange pound cake, there is no dessert more special. It's slightly different from ordinary chocolate sauce because of its delightful orange undertones.

Makes about 2 cups

8 ounces (8 squares) semisweet chocolate
⅓ cup fresh orange juice, strained
2 tablespoons (¼ stick) unsalted butter, at
    room temperature
¾ cup heavy cream
1 to 2 teaspoons orange liqueur

1. In the top of a double boiler over medium heat, melt the chocolate with the orange juice.

2. Remove the double boiler from the heat and stir the chocolate until smooth. Swirl in the butter.

3. Heat the cream and stir into the chocolate mixture along with the orange liqueur. Serve hot or warm.

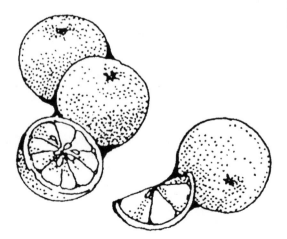

CHANTILLY CREAM

Makes 1½ cups

1 cup whipping cream
½ teaspoon vanilla extract
1 teaspoon orange liqueur or cognac
1 to 3 tablespoons sugar
2 tablespoons sour cream

1. Place the cream in a medium bowl and refrigerate until very cold. Place the beaters of an electric mixer in the freezer until very cold.

2. Beat the cream for 1 minute with the electric mixer at medium speed.

3. Add the vanilla and the liqueur, and beat just to combine. Pour in the sugar and beat at medium speed for about 2 minutes or until very soft peaks form.

4. Add the sour cream and continue beating until fluffy and well combined. Do not overbeat. This type of cream should be very soft, almost pourable.

RASPBERRY SAUCE

With vanilla ice cream!

Makes about 1 cup

1 (12-ounce) package frozen raspberries, thawed; or 3 cups fresh raspberries
2 tablespoons confectioners' sugar
1 teaspoon lemon juice, or more to taste
2 teaspoons framboise (raspberry liqueur)

1. Purée the raspberries in a blender until smooth.

2. Add the sugar, lemon juice and liqueur. Blend again briefly. Strain the sauce. Serve at room temperature.

MIXED BERRIES SAUCE In a medium sauté pan, heat 2 tablespoons water and 3 tablespoons sugar, stirring constantly until dissolved. Add 2 teaspoons fresh lemon juice and ½ cup each cut strawberries, blueberries, and blackberries; cook the sauce over medium heat for 2 to 3 minutes. Cool to room temperature before serving.

COGNAC CRÈME ANGLAISE

A classic custard sauce that seems to beg for a chocolate cake, layered with mousse and topped with chocolate shavings.

Makes about 2½ cups

6 egg yolks, at room temperature
⅓ cup light brown sugar, firmly packed
Pinch of salt
2 cups half-and-half
¼ cup cognac

1. In a metal bowl, whisk together the egg yolks, brown sugar and salt. Whisk in the half-and-half a little at a time.

2. Place the bowl over simmering water, stirring constantly with a wooden spoon until the custard is done. (To test for doneness, dip the wooden spoon in the custard and draw a finger across the back of the spoon. If a clear path is left in the custard, it is done. Do not boil.)

3. Strain into a bowl. Cool, then stir in the cognac.

NOTE Serve this sauce warm or cold. To cool quickly, place the bowl of custard in a larger bowl filled with ice cubes. Stir until it reaches the desired temperature.

CHOCOLATE CRÈME ANGLAISE
Instead of light brown sugar, use 3 tablespoons granulated sugar. Grate 2 ounces (2 squares) semisweet chocolate. Add the chocolate after the crème Anglaise has started to thicken slightly.

DRESSINGS

Unlike any other "uncooked" element in food preparation, the dressing for a salad lends a unique opportunity for creativity. Simply add oil, an acid and a flavoring such as mustard or herbs to give a dressing distinction.

A dressing can grant a salad personality: aggressive, laid-back, mild, strong, interesting, unexpected. If a rule exists with regard to dressing a salad, it is this: first-course salads are usually simple, and their dressing should be simple, too, with greater emphasis on the acid—lighter vinegars or lemon juice. They should stimulate the palate and encourage the appetite. When a salad is served as a main course, the only limitation is your imagination. With last-course salads, or digestives (not typical on this side of the Atlantic), go very light on the dressing, especially the amount of acid, since these are salads meant to settle the stomach rather than stimulate the appetite. In every case, always use the best ingredients.

DRESSING BASICS

A FEW WORDS ABOUT OIL

The foundation of a good dressing is the oil. Just as there are many different salads, so there are many different oils to use in a dressing. Extra-virgin olive oil can, to a great degree, be considered the most important oil for a dressing. Recent experimentation with nut oils has brought them into more common use, hazelnut and walnut oil being among the most widely accepted and available. Oils labeled just "vegetable oil" should not be used in dressings, since they add no flavor and bring along with them a collection of unwanted chemicals.

ALMOND OIL: With the delicate and flavorful taste of almonds. Use sparingly.

AVOCADO OIL: Generally a light taste. It mixes very well with flavored vinegars such as sherry, pear and balsamic; delicate greens are complemented perfectly with this oil.

DARK (ORIENTAL) SESAME OIL: A rich, dark oil made from toasted sesame seeds, with an intense flavor. It should be diluted with milder oils, such as light sesame oil or safflower oil.

HAZELNUT OIL: A rich, nutty flavor. It mixes well with mellow vinegars, and a little goes a long way.

OLIVE OIL: Always look for "cold press" process. Other notations on the label, like "extra-virgin, "virgin" and "pure," which correspond with the first, second and third pressings of the olives, refer to the acidity level in the oil. Note the difference among these three distinctions: *extra-virgin* is a "cold pressed" oil from the finest hand-picked olives, extracted from the first pressing; *virgin olive oil* is from lower-quality olives and can be derived from subsequent pressings with the use of heat and hydraulic presses; *pure olive oil* is the product of pulp, ground skins and pits, with the oil sometimes even removed by chemical methods.

Besides Italian, French, Greek and Spanish olive oils, some very good California oils are now available. Cooking with olive oil is different from serving the oil uncooked in a dressing: grades lower than extra-virgin may successfully be used for sautéing and frying.

SAFFLOWER OIL: A good, pure oil for lighter dressings or to tone down stronger-tasting oils. It is flavorless and has no cholesterol.

SESAME OIL: Light, almost flavorless. It is good for simple dressings or those where olive oil would add too much flavor, especially dressings that are sweet.

WALNUT OIL: Delicate but with a definite walnut taste. Mix with light wine vinegars, and use sparingly or combine with safflower oil.

STORING FINE OILS: Always store oils in a cool, dark place in a tightly covered container. Olive oil keeps for only one year after it has been opened, not longer. Nut oils have an even shorter shelf life—about three months—so it is wise to indicate the date the oil was opened on the container.

FLAVORED OLIVE OILS: For flavored oils, use extra-virgin olive oil. To prepare, place the ingredients in a glass jar and cover with 4 cups extra-virgin olive oil, leaving 1¼-inches space on top. Cover and allow to marinate ten days before using. (A wine bottle with a cork is a good container to use.) Try any of the following combinations:
• Rosemary-garlic: 3 sprigs fresh rosemary and 2 unpeeled garlic cloves, slashed
• Thyme: 4 (5-inch) sprigs thyme and 2 bay leaves (optional)
• Pepper-oregano: 16 black peppercorns; 8 coriander seeds and 3 (3-inch) oregano sprigs
• Southwest: 2 small dried red chiles
• Porcini mushroom: 1 ounce large dried porcini (rinsed and well drained) and 10 black peppercorns

A FEW WORDS ABOUT OTHER INGREDIENTS

VINEGAR: Red wine, white wine, Champagne, sherry and balsamic vinegars are the basics and the best. Herb- and fruit-scented vinegars are available, though higher priced, at gourmet specialty stores and more frequently in the grocery store. Cider, white and malt vinegars are generally too tart for salad dressings, thus overpowering the delicate balance of the ingredients. As with oils, only the best vinegars should be used in making dressings.

The best French vinegars are from Orléans, in the Loire region of France. California wine vinegars are now widely available as well. Almost all Italian red wine vinegars are dry and of good quality. Avoid vinegars that are pasteurized or that include additives or chemicals. Cloudiness is not an indication of bad vinegar. It sometimes occurs with unpasteurized wine vinegars, and can be eliminated by heating the vinegar to a boil, then returning it to the bottle.

HONEY: The ideal sweetener for dressing, honey dissolves immediately in liquids and brings out many other subtle flavors in even the most delicate dressings. Honey should be used sparingly, since it is very sweet.

HERBS—PRESERVED IN OIL: After a summer of inventive salads drizzled with creative and interesting dressings, think about putting away some of the harvest from your precious herb garden (or herbs bought in bunches from the country market) for the seasons to come.

In a blender, purée 1 cup of fresh herbs in ¼ cup of olive oil. They will keep for months in covered containers. Mint, thyme, tarragon, rosemary, oregano, basil—all you need is a couple of teaspoons of these herbs added to a dressing or sauce.

FINALLY A LITTLE "MEAT" IN THE PRODUCE DEPARTMENT

In a manner of speaking. A lot of new shapes, colors, textures and tastes are cropping up in the vegetable department. And not just in gourmet grocery stores, either. Here are some of the more interesting selections that you might want to look for.

ARUGULA: It is a member of the mustard family with a delicate peppery taste and a distinctive tartness. Eat very young arugula; its flavor turns bitter with age. Many types of dressings taste good with arugula, from a simple vinaigrette to a more substantial dressing like Creamy Basil.

ASPARAGUS: The delicate vegetable should always be trimmed to about 5 inches before cooking. Blanch a dozen or so of the wandlike vegetables and drizzle on Creamy Garlic Dressing after the asparagus has been well chilled.

AVOCADOS: There's nothing new or exotic about this fruit consumed year-round in the manner of a vegetable—with a dash of salt, pepper and lemon juice. Glorious green guacamole, everyone's favorite Mexican dip, is made with avocados. This everyday delicacy has a smooth, rich, nutlike flavor.

BELGIAN ENDIVE: Belgian endive is one of the world's most costly vegetables, but only a few of the slightly bitter-tasting leaves are required to zip up a salad; or serve a few of the leaves lightly dressed in Raspberry Vinaigrette as an elegant side salad.

BOK CHOY: Once found primarily in the restaurant kitchens of Chinatown and now almost as common as big green cabbage, its flavor—faintly reminiscent of water chestnuts—offers a wonderful way to give American coleslaw an interesting oriental slant.

CHAYOTE SQUASH: In shape and color, it is similar to a papaya, but has one large seed. Chayote has become popular as a grilling vegetable. Diced or grated raw, it makes a hearty addition to mixed vegetable salads. Choose a strong dressing, like Creamy Tarragon.

DAIKON: This Japanese white radish is juicy, with a mildly peppery flavor. Typically, it is grated and served as a bed for sashimi (raw fish). Serve daikon in a side salad that features other oriental ingredients, and dress it with a creamy dressing.

ENOKI MUSHROOMS: This Japanese vegetable has a crisp, mild flavor, perfect with mixed green salads. Oriental Vinaigrette is a natural when it comes to the choice of dressing.

JICAMA: Primarily from Mexico, where it is served raw as an appetizer with a squeeze of fresh lime juice, pepper and salt. Jicama has a crisp, refreshing sweetness that lends crunch and flavor to fruit and vegetable salads. A poppy seed dressing makes an interesting partner.

RADICCHIO: The price of this ruby-red and-white wild chicory—often $5 a pound or more—is due to its long and unpredictable growing time. A radicchio salad with shredded Parmesan cheese and Creamy Balsamic Vinaigrette possesses the most interesting taste imaginable.

SPROUTS: Sprouts of beans or seeds, a true Asian delicacy, are today standard salad fare, adding interesting taste, texture and even protein. Mix all types together—mung beans, radish and alfalfa sprouts. Place on a bed of curly red-leaf lettuce and drizzle on a Dijon Vinaigrette.

SWEET PEPPERS: There are many colors to choose from: green (actually an unripened red pepper), red, purple and yellow. All are sweet and are related to the hot chile.

TOMATOES: Buy only vine-ripened tomatoes; their taste, texture and color make other tomatoes pale in every way. For contrast in a simple lettuce and vine-ripened tomato salad, dress the ingredients with Pesto Vinaigrette and top with toasted pine nuts.

WATERCRESS: The most common type actually belongs to the nasturtium family. It's an excellent salad ingredient served in combination with milder lettuces and other greens. Drizzle on Champagne Vinaigrette and top with cracked black pepper.

DRESSING A SALAD IN THE ITALIAN FASHION

Italians always put it on at the table! Place the washed, dried and crisped lettuce in a bowl twice as large as the amount of lettuce. Drizzle on extra-virgin olive oil, then the best quality wine vinegar—flavored or unflavored, red or white, or a combination of Italian dry red wine vinegar and a few drops of balsamic vinegar. Season with a sprinkling of salt, several turns of the pepper mill and 1 teaspoon or more dried basil. Toss to combine well. Top each portion with another twist of the pepper mill, if desired.

THE DRESSING MAKER'S PANTRY

Always have these items within arm's reach for making a perfect dressing. Buy the best-quality ingredients—it makes all the difference in the taste.

ACIDS
Fresh lemon juice
Fresh lime juice
Vinegars: herb-flavored, red wine, white wine, fruit-flavored, balsamic, sherry

HERBS AND SPICES
Herbes de Provence
Fresh and dried herbs: chervil, dill, mint, tarragon, basil, marjoram, thyme.
Ground spices: cinnamon, nutmeg, coriander, ginger
White and black peppercorns, sea salt

OILS
Light sesame
Dark sesame
Safflower
Extra-virgin olive
Walnut or hazelnut

VINAIGRETTES

SCALLION VINAIGRETTE

Makes about 1 cup

1 teaspoon Dijon-style mustard
1 teaspoon lemon juice
½ cup extra-virgin olive oil
2 bunches scallions (white parts and some of the green), finely chopped
Salt and freshly ground black pepper

1. Combine the mustard and lemon juice. Whisk in the olive oil in a thin stream.

2. Stir in the scallions and season to taste with salt and pepper. Allow to stand at room temperature for 1 hour before using. Whisk before pouring.

SHALLOT VINAIGRETTE Instead of scallions, add 3 large shallots, finely chopped; and instead of lemon juice, use 1 tablespoon white wine vinegar.

CORIANDER VINAIGRETTE

Makes about 1 cup

1 teaspoon coriander seeds
2 tablespoons sherry vinegar
¾ teaspoon Dijon-style mustard
2 tablespoons safflower oil
¼ cup extra-virgin olive oil
½ small red onion, very thinly sliced
Salt

1. In a small skillet over medium heat, cook the coriander seeds, stirring continuously for about 2 minutes. When they become fragrant, remove from the heat.

2. With a mortar and pestle or a spice grinder, grind the seeds to a powder.

3. In a small bowl, whisk together the coriander, vinegar and mustard. Add the oils in a thin stream, whisking constantly until the ingredients are thoroughly combined.

4. Add the onion and salt to taste. Stir before pouring.

DIJON VINAIGRETTE

Makes about ¾ cup

¼ cup Italian red wine vinegar
1 tablespoon Dijon-style mustard
1 teaspoon honey
½ teaspoon freshly ground black pepper
Pinch of salt
2 tablespoons safflower oil

⅓ cup extra-virgin olive oil
1 tablespoon chopped fresh chives
1 teaspoon dried herbs

1. In a small bowl, combine all the ingredients. Whisk to mix well.

2. Allow to stand 1 hour. Whisk before pouring.

MINT VINAIGRETTE

Makes 1 cup

½ cup extra-virgin olive oil
½ cup fine white wine vinegar
½ teaspoon Dijon-style mustard
3 tablespoons finely minced fresh mint
1 tablespoon finely chopped fresh parsley
Pinch of salt
Pinch of sugar

1. In a jar with a tight-fitting cover, combine the ingredients. Mix well by shaking.

2. Allow to stand at room temperature for 30 minutes. Shake before pouring.

CINNAMON VINAIGRETTE

Makes about ¾ cup

3 tablespoons safflower oil
3 tablespoons Champagne or white wine
    vinegar
⅓ cup juice from canned mandarin orange
    segments

Salt
¼ teaspoon freshly ground white pepper
2 tablespoons ground cinnamon

1. In a jar with a tight-fitting cover, combine the ingredients. Mix well by shaking.

2. Shake again before pouring.

SHERRY VINAIGRETTE

Makes 1 cup

¼ cup extra-virgin olive oil
½ cup sherry vinegar
¼ cup walnut oil
1 teaspoon chopped shallot

1. In a small bowl, combine the ingredients. Whisk to mix well.

2. Whisk before pouring.

BASIL LIME VINAIGRETTE

Makes about 1⅔ cups

1 cup fresh basil leaves, firmly packed
1 tablespoon fresh lime juice
1½ teaspoons white wine vinegar
½ teaspoon Dijon-style mustard
1 small garlic clove
½ cup extra-virgin olive oil
Salt and freshly ground black pepper

1. In a blender or food processor fitted with a steel blade, combine the basil, lime juice, vinegar, mustard and garlic. With the motor running, add the oil in a thin, steady stream. Season to taste with salt and pepper.

2. Refrigerate until needed. Whisk before pouring.

CAESAR VINAIGRETTE

Makes about 1¼ cups

3 tablespoons white wine vinegar
1 tablespoon Dijon-style mustard
Pinch of salt
½ cup extra-virgin olive oil
1 teaspoon anchovy paste, or 2 anchovy filets, rinsed and finely chopped
1 tablespoon small capers, drained
1 egg yolk, lightly beaten with ¼ teaspoon water

½ cup freshly grated Parmesan cheese

1. In a small bowl, combine the vinegar, mustard and salt. Whisk to mix well.

2. Whisk in the olive oil in a thin stream.

3. Whisk in the anchovy, capers, and egg yolk until well combined. Stir in the Parmesan cheese. Serve immediately.

ORIENTAL VINAIGRETTE

Makes about ½ cup

¼ cup light sesame oil
2 tablespoons dark sesame oil
3 tablespoons rice vinegar
2 tablespoons light soy sauce
1 teaspoon grated fresh ginger
Freshly ground white pepper
1 tablespoon toasted sesame seeds, for
    garnish

1. In a small bowl, combine all the ingredients except the sesame seeds. Whisk to mix well.

2. Whisk before pouring. Top the salad with the sesame seeds.

PESTO VINAIGRETTE

Makes about ¾ cup

½ cup Pesto (page 29)
3 tablespoons white wine vinegar
3 tablespoons extra-virgin olive oil

1. In a small bowl, combine the ingredients. Whisk to mix well.

2. Whisk before pouring.

HAZELNUT OIL VINAIGRETTE

Makes about ½ cup

3 tablespoons hazelnut oil
3 tablespoons extra-virgin olive oil
2 tablespoons white wine vinegar
¼ teaspoon salt
⅛ teaspoon finely ground white pepper

1. In a small bowl, combine all the ingredients. Whisk to mix well.

2. Whisk before pouring.

WALNUT OIL VINAIGRETTE Substitute walnut oil for hazelnut oil, and sherry vinegar for white wine vinegar. Continue as directed.

CHAMPAGNE VINAIGRETTE

Makes about 1½ cups

1 cup extra-virgin olive oil, or ½ cup safflower oil and ½ cup extra-virgin olive oil
⅓ cup Champagne vinegar
Salt
½ teaspoon freshly ground white pepper
1½ tablespoons fresh lemon juice
½ teaspoon sugar

1. In a jar with a tight-fitting cover, combine the ingredients. Mix well by shaking.

2. Allow to stand at room temperature for 1 hour. Shake before pouring.

BLUEBERRY VINAIGRETTE

Makes about 1 cup

½ cup extra-virgin olive oil
½ cup blueberry wine vinegar
Pinch of salt
1 teaspoon freshly ground white pepper
½ cup fresh blueberries

1. In a jar with a tight-fitting cover, combine the ingredients. Mix well by shaking.

2. Allow to stand at room temperature for 1 to 2 hours. Strain the fruit and shake the dressing again before pouring.

RASPBERRY VINAIGRETTE Substitute raspberry vinegar and raspberries (fresh or frozen) for blueberry vinegar and blueberries. Continue as directed.

MANGO VINAIGRETTE

Makes about 1¼ cups

2 tablespoons dark sesame oil
2 tablespoons rice vinegar
1 ripe mango, peeled, seeded and cut into
    chunks
½ teaspoon curry powder

1. In a blender or food processor fitted with a steel blade, combine all the ingredients and process until smooth. Refrigerate, covered, until needed.

2. Stir before pouring.

FRESH TOMATO VINAIGRETTE

Makes about 2½ cups

1 shallot, finely minced
⅓ cup sherry vinegar
2 sprigs tarragon
1 tablespoon tomato paste
¼ cup water
1 large ripe tomato, peeled, seeded and
      quartered
½ cup extra-virgin olive oil

1 cup tomato juice (unsalted)
1 teaspoon salt
½ teaspoon freshly ground black pepper

1. Place all the ingredients in a blender. Blend until well mixed. Place the dressing in a jar with a tight-fitting cover.

2. Refrigerate until needed. Shake again before pouring.

LEMON HERB DRESSING

Makes ¾ cup

¼ cup extra-virgin olive oil
⅓ cup lemon juice
½ small garlic clove, finely minced
1 teaspoon salt
½ teaspoon freshly ground black pepper
1 tablespoon finely chopped fresh parsley

1 tablespoon finely chopped fresh tarragon
1 tablespoon finely chopped fresh chives
1 tablespoon finely chopped fresh basil

1. In a jar with a tight-fitting lid, combine the oil, lemon juice, garlic, salt and pepper. Shake until the ingredients thicken.

2. Stir in the herbs just before serving.

ORANGE VINAIGRETTE

Makes about 1 cup

3 tablespoons fresh orange juice
¼ cup Champagne vinegar
2 teaspoons grated orange zest, blanched
½ cup extra-virgin olive oil

1. In a small bowl, combine the orange juice, vinegar and orange zest. Whisk in the olive oil in a thin stream.

2. Refrigerate until needed. Whisk before pouring.

PINK GRAPEFRUIT VINAIGRETTE
Use pink grapefruit juice and grated lemon zest instead of orange juice and zest. Use some of the grapefruit in the salad.

ORANGE DRESSING

Makes about ⅓ cup

3 tablespoons orange juice
1 tablespoon Champagne vinegar
1 teaspoon lemon juice
⅛ teaspoon salt
⅛ teaspoon freshly ground black pepper
1 tablespoon extra-virgin olive oil
1 tablespoon balsamic vinegar

1. In a small bowl, combine all the ingredients. Whisk to mix well.

2. Whisk before pouring.

LOW-CALORIE DRESSINGS

LEMON CHIVE DRESSING

Makes about ½ cup

¼ cup fresh lemon juice
2 tablespoons chopped fresh chives
2 tablespoons minced shallots
2 teaspoons Dijon-style mustard
Salt and freshly ground black pepper

1. In a blender, combine all the ingredients. Blend at high speed until smooth.

2. Refrigerate 1 hour. Stir before pouring.

CREAMY GREEN HERB DRESSING

Makes about 2¼ cups

2 tablespoons Italian (flat-leaf) parsley leaves
2 tablespoons fresh dill weed, packed
¼ cup watercress leaves, packed
¼ cup packed spinach leaves, blanched,
    drained and dried
1½ cups low-fat cottage cheese
¼ cup low-fat milk
Salt and freshly ground black pepper

1. In a food processor fitted with a steel blade, process the parsley, dill and watercress until well chopped. Remove to a small bowl and set aside.

2. Chop the spinach in a food processor. Add to the herbs.

3. Blend the cottage cheese at high speed until smooth. Add milk as needed to attain a creamy, pourable consistency.

4. Fold the herb and spinach mixture into the cottage cheese. Season to taste with salt and pepper.

5. Refrigerate, covered, until needed. Stir before serving.

CREAMY CURRY DRESSING

Makes about 1½ cups

1 cup low-fat cottage cheese
3 tablespoons skim milk
1 tablespoon curry powder (Madras, if possible)
2 tablespoons safflower or other light vegetable oil
2 teaspoons fresh lemon juice
1 teaspoon honey
2 to 4 tablespoons Major Grey's chutney
Salt and freshly ground white pepper

1. In a blender or food processor fitted with a steel blade, combine the cottage cheese and milk. Process until smooth. Add the curry powder and process until well combined and no lumps of curry powder are visible.

2. With the machine running, add the oil in a thin stream. Transfer the dressing to a small bowl.

3. Stir in the lemon juice, honey and chutney. Mix well. Add salt and pepper to taste. Refrigerate, covered, until needed. Stir before serving.

GRAPEFRUIT DRESSING

Makes about ⅓ cup

¼ cup fresh grapefruit juice
1 teaspoon walnut oil
1 tablespoon chicken stock

1. In a small bowl, combine all the ingredients. Whisk to mix well.

2. Whisk before pouring.

LEMON OR LIME DRESSING Substitute lemon or lime juice for grapefruit juice. Add 2 teaspoons honey or artificial sweetener to taste. Use safflower oil instead of walnut oil. Add 1 teaspoon Dijon-style mustard. Eliminate the chicken stock.

POPPY SEED DRESSING (FOR FRUIT SALADS)

Makes about 2 cups

1 cup plain yogurt
2 ripe bananas
2 tablespoons lemon or lime juice
2 tablespoons honey
1 teaspoon Champagne vinegar
2 tablespoons poppy seeds

1. In a blender or food processor fitted with a steel blade, combine all the ingredients except the poppy seeds. Process until smooth. Stir in the poppy seeds.

2. Refrigerate until needed. Stir before serving.

POPPY SEED DRESSING (FOR VEGETABLE SALADS)

Just a tablespoon of this dressing tossed with crisp, blanched vegetables makes a delicious, low-calorie lunch.

Makes about 1½ cups

2 tablespoons dry white wine
2 tablespoons dry mustard
⅓ cup Champagne vinegar
2 tablespoons finely chopped shallots
2 tablespoons poppy seeds
¼ teaspoon salt
¼ teaspoon freshly ground white pepper
⅔ cup extra-virgin olive oil

1. In a small bowl, whisk together the wine and mustard. Let stand for 15 minutes.

2. In a medium bowl, combine the mustard mixture, vinegar, shallots, poppy seeds, salt and pepper. Whisk in the oil in a thin stream. Store in a covered container in the refrigerator for up to two weeks.

TOMATO HERB DRESSING

Makes about ¾ cup

1 (6-ounce) can low-sodium tomato or vegetable juice
Juice of 1 lemon
¼ teaspoon dried basil (or other herbs)
¼ to 1 teaspoon salt-free seasoning

1. In a jar with a tight-fitting lid, combine all the ingredients. Shake to mix well.

2. Refrigerate 1 hour. Shake before pouring.

TAHINI DRESSING (SESAME)

Makes about 2½ cups

½ cup safflower oil
½ pound tofu, drained
¼ cup fresh lemon juice
¼ cup tahini (sesame paste)
1 garlic clove, minced
½ cup cold water
½ teaspoon salt

1 scallion (white parts and some of the
  green), chopped

1. In a blender or food processor fitted with a steel blade, combine all the ingredients except the scallions. Process until smooth. If the dressing is too thick, add a little more water.

2. Stir in the scallions. Refrigerate, covered. Stir before serving.

YOGURT DILL DRESSING

Makes about ½ cup

½ cup plain yogurt
2 teaspoons fresh lemon juice, or more to
  taste
¼ teaspoon grated lemon zest
2 teaspoons finely chopped fresh dill (stems
  removed)

1. In a small bowl, combine all the ingredients. Whisk to mix well. Refrigerate for 1 hour.

2. Whisk before pouring.

CAPER DRESSING Instead of the dill, add 2 teaspoons capers, drained, rinsed and slightly crushed.

TART YOGURT DRESSING

Makes about ½ cup

½ cup plain yogurt
2 tablespoons orange juice, or 1 tablespoon
  lemon juice mixed with 1 teaspoon
  honey
1 teaspoon Dijon-style mustard

1. In a blender, combine all the ingredients. Blend well.

2. Refrigerate for 1 hour. Whisk before pouring.

YOGURT MINT DRESSING

Makes about 3 cups

1 cup plain yogurt
1 cup cottage cheese
½ cup fresh mint leaves, firmly packed
1 teaspoon ground cumin
¼ teaspoon salt
⅓ cup light vegetable oil, such as safflower
¼ cup fresh lemon juice

1. In a blender, combine the yogurt and cottage cheese. Blend until smooth.

2. Add the mint, cumin, salt, oil and lemon juice; continue blending just until smooth. (Mint will appear as flecks in the dressing.)

3. Refrigerate until needed. Stir before serving.

CREAMY DRESSINGS

CREAMY GARLIC DRESSING

Makes about 1 cup

2 garlic cloves, minced
1 egg
3 tablespoons Chardonnay wine vinegar
Salt and freshly ground white pepper
½ cup extra-virgin olive oil

1. In a blender or food processor, blend the garlic, egg, vinegar, salt, pepper and 1 tablespoon of the olive oil.

2. With the motor running, add the remaining olive oil in a thin stream until well combined and creamy. Refrigerate until needed. Stir before pouring.

ROQUEFORT DRESSING

Makes about 2 cups

½ cup heavy cream
½ cup crème frâiche or sour cream
1 teaspoon (or less) Worcestershire sauce
¼ teaspoon salt
½ teaspoon freshly ground white pepper
1 to 1½ cups Roquefort cheese
¼ cup milk

1. In a blender or food processor, combine the cream, crème frâiche or sour cream, Worcestershire sauce, salt and pepper. Process until combined.

2. Add the Roquefort and blend just to combine; the dressing should be chunky. Stir in the milk to thin the dressing; add more if necessary.

3. Refrigerate, covered, for at least 2 hours. Stir before serving.

CREAMY BALSAMIC VINAIGRETTE

Makes about 1¼ cups

1 tablespoon Dijon-style mustard
3 tablespoons balsamic vinegar
Salt and freshly ground black pepper
¾ cup extra-virgin olive oil
3 tablespoons heavy cream
1 garlic clove, cut in half

1. In a small bowl, whisk together the mustard and the balsamic vinegar. Season to taste with salt and pepper.

2. Whisk in the olive oil in a thin stream. Add the cream and continue whisking until well combined and the dressing is creamy.

3. Add the garlic halves and allow to stand, covered, for 1 hour or more. Remove the garlic. Whisk before pouring.

BALSAMIC: THE MYSTERIOUS AGED VINEGAR

Balsamic vinegar was known as the gift of Gods—or so it was back in the eleventh century. Dukes offered it to their honored guests. Bonificio presented it to Emperor Arrigo IV.

Balsamic vinegar is made only in Modena, where the climate is just right for growing the Trebbiano de Spanga grapes. The grapes are slowly cooked for hours, producing the grape "must," which is aged in wood casks made of chestnut, oak, juniper or mulberry. Each year the vinegar is decanted from a bigger cask to smaller ones made from a different wood. The casks, which are handed down from generation to generation, are kept in warm, airy, humidity-free attics for aging. The result of this patient, arduous labor is a vinegar of rich burgundy color, exquisite aroma and delicate flavor that cannot be reproduced anywhere in the world.

Always use this sparingly, since the mellow, reddish brown vinegar is very flavorful.

CREAMY TARRAGON DRESSING

Makes about 1½ cups

5 tablespoons tarragon vinegar
½ teaspoon salt
1 teaspoon freshly ground black pepper
½ teaspoon Dijon-style mustard
1 garlic clove, minced
⅔ cup extra-virgin olive oil
1 small egg, lightly beaten
⅓ cup half-and-half
2 teaspoons chopped fresh tarragon

1. In a small bowl, whisk together the vinegar, salt, pepper, mustard and garlic.

2. Add the olive oil in a thin stream, whisking vigorously until well combined.

3. Combine the egg and half-and-half. Whisk into the dressing until thoroughly combined and creamy.

4. Stir in the tarragon. Refrigerate until needed. Stir before pouring.

CREAMY HERB DRESSING

Makes about 1 cup

6 ounces cream cheese, at room temperature
¼ cup sour cream
¼ cup herb-scented wine vinegar
1 tablespoon fresh chopped marjoram
1 tablespoon chopped fresh parsley
1 tablespoon chopped fresh chives
1 tablespoon chopped fresh basil
2 teaspoons minced garlic
1 tablespoon milk, or more if needed
Salt and freshly ground black pepper

1. In a blender, combine all the ingredients. Blend until smooth. Add more milk if the dressing is too thick; it should be thick but a pourable consistency.

2. Refrigerate until needed. Stir before serving.

BUTTERMILK DRESSING

Makes about ½ cup

¼ cup buttermilk
2 tablespoons white wine vinegar
¼ cup extra-virgin olive oil
1 to 2 drops Tabasco
¼ teaspoon celery seed
⅛ teaspoon Worcestershire sauce
Salt and freshly ground black pepper

1. In a small bowl, combine the buttermilk and the vinegar. Add the oil in a thin, steady stream, whisking until thoroughly combined and creamy.

2. Whisk in the Tabasco, celery seed, Worcestershire sauce and salt and pepper. Whisk before pouring.

CREAMY GORGONZOLA DRESSING

Makes about 1¼ cups

½ cup extra-virgin olive oil
6 tablespoons white wine vinegar
¼ cup plain yogurt
½ teaspoon Dijon-style mustard
½ cup crumbled Gorgonzola cheese
Salt and freshly ground white pepper

1. In a small bowl, whisk the oil, vinegar, yogurt, and mustard together until well combined. Whisk in the Gorgonzola, salt and pepper.

2. Refrigerate until needed. Stir before serving.

NOTE Roquefort or Stilton may be substituted for Gorgonzola.

CREAMY CUCUMBER DRESSING

Makes about 2½ cups

1 cucumber, peeled, halved, seeded and grated
½ cup sour cream
½ cup heavy cream
¼ cup chopped fresh herbs (parsley, tarragon, basil, mint, dill or chives, or a combination)
Salt and freshly ground white pepper
Chopped pimiento, for garnish

1. Press the cucumber into a strainer to remove the liquid.

2. In a medium bowl, mix the cucumber, sour cream, cream, herbs, salt and pepper.

3. Refrigerate until needed. Stir before serving. Garnish with pimiento.

CREAMY BASIL DRESSING

Makes about 2¼ cups

¼ cup white wine vinegar
2 tablespoons Dijon-style mustard
1 egg yolk
2 garlic cloves
⅓ cup light vegetable oil
1 cup sour cream
½ cup fresh chopped basil
Salt and freshly ground white pepper
Chopped chives, for garnish

1. In a blender or food processor fitted with a steel blade, combine the vinegar, mustard, egg yolk and garlic. Blend or process just until smooth.

2. With the machine running, add the oil in a thin stream. Continue blending until the dressing is well combined and creamy.

3. Add the sour cream and blend just until combined. Transfer the dressing to a bowl and fold in the chopped basil, salt and pepper to taste.

4. Refrigerate, covered, until needed. Stir before serving. Garnish with chives.

INDEX

93